Pure Bliss in La Boca

A history of Boca Juniors and the passion in La Bombonera

PURE BLISS IN LA BOCA: A HISTORY OF BOCA JUNIORS AND THE PASSION IN LA BOMBONERA

First edition. July 28, 2025.

Copyright © 2025 Rob Smith.

ISBN: 979-8231778607

Written by Rob Smith.

Dedicated to my family.

By Rob Smith

FOREWORD by Mariano Valdés.

Boca es Boca

My friend Rob has entrusted me with a difficult task: to summarize, in a prologue, what Boca means and why the existence of this book is so important. A book that not only provides truthful and verified content (so vital in the era of fake news and the imminent threat of a post-truth world driven by artificial intelligence), but also captures the soul of a phenomenon. At first glance, this might seem like an impossible mission. Fortunately, Boca fans already have the answer. To my English-speaking friends: don't expect a long-winded explanation. The answer is right there in the title of this prologue. **Boca is Boca.**

What does that second "Boca" mean? Everything.

Boca Juniors, a non-profit sports association, is much more than an institution. It's about people—its people. It's a social phenomenon (and without exaggeration, I would say it's the most passionate in human history) that transcends all borders: from the humble neighborhood of La Boca, to the rest of Argentina, to the Americas. And though empirical evidence is yet to be found, I predict it will one day cross the boundaries of planet Earth and the Milky Way.

This phenomenon is built upon core values: love for the club, for our beloved neighbourhood, for our grassroots origins. It's about unwavering support for the team (which only intensifies when times are tough), pride in our Bombonera, the need to sing and embrace fellow Boca fans, and a set of feelings that cannot be easily explained—but are deeply felt.

So what is this "Boca," really? It's a blend of values forged through shared history, through hard times and epic feats—both sporting and cultural. It's in the celebrations. It's in the way Boca fans express love for their club, matched only by the hatred (mainly) of rival fans—and, in many cases, their admiration. It's about a humble origin, paired with an unlimited desire to grow and welcome anyone who understands what we are, no matter where or when they were born.

It's more than a club. It's a way of life: **Boca is our way of life.**

That's why it's no surprise that my friend Rob—born in Ireland, with no direct or indirect ties to Argentine history or culture—decided to become a Boca fan. *"Somos soldados de La Bombonera,"* he often says, in Spanish with a Saxon accent, but with perfect use of the first-person plural: *"Somos"* / *"We are."*

How did we meet? That could be another book entirely. Just one more anecdote in Boca's rich history—which I invite you to explore in the pages ahead.

Thank you, my friend. I'm proud to have contributed to your book.

Boca IS Boca.

—MARIANO VALDÉS
President, Consulado Boca Juniors Mallorca (2020–2025).

Active Member of Club Atlético Boca Juniors.

Alternate Assembly Member, Assembly of Representatives of Club Atlético Boca Juniors (2023–2027) — the first ever elected while residing outside Argentina.

Member, Foreign Affairs Committee of the Department of Interior and Foreign Affairs of Club Atlético Boca Juniors.

Friend of Rob Smith and resident of Valldemossa (Mallorca), Spain.

INTRODUCTION

Some stadiums have a natural gravitational force. They just do. For example, if a football fan finds themselves in the city of Milan, they will very likely make a pilgrimage to see the epic San Siro. The same can be said for Barcelona with the Camp Nou, Dortmund's Westfalenstadion or Liverpool with the historic Anfield.

Why do the fans feel a strong attraction to visit these cathedrals of sporting greatness? To experience the sense of history and the thousands upon thousands of nights where thousands upon thousands of people have gone before them to feel the elation or devastation in watching their team take to the sacred field? To be close to the pitch where numerous icons of the beautiful game have given blood, sweat and tears to produce magic? Or perhaps to simply say "I was there"?

There are bucket list stadiums for most football fans. And there is one that is continually on most football fans' list, right up the top, and it lies in the neighbourhood of La Boca, in Buenos Aires, Argentina.

When you walk away from Plaza de Mayo in the centre of the city, heading south on the Avenida Paseo Colón, eventually you'll come to the leafy Parque Lezama, a lovely city park in the San Telmo neighbourhood. From there, you'll be able to see Avenida Almirante Brown, named after the Irish-born William Brown, founder of the Argentine navy. It is here that you have entered La Boca.

Keep walking down Av. Brown until you come to Brandsen on the right, a narrow city street in the heart of the neighbourhood. Eventually as you continue to walk down this street, the colours on the walls become increasingly visible. All you will see is blue and yellow. On one wall, you'll read *Boca Nunca Teme Luchar* (Boca is never afraid to fight). You'll also see murals to some of La Boca's other attractions, such as the *Puente transbordador Nicolás Avellaneda*, an old transporter bridge which lies mere blocks away that is now a National Historic Monument for Argentina. Now the yellow and blue are becoming more prominent. You won't see much red around here, the colours of bitter rivals River Plate. It is strictly yellow and blue in this *barrio* and especially on Brandsen.

And there it is to your right. The temple, La Bombonera.

CHAPTER ONE

At the turn of the 20th century, Buenos Aires was a rapidly growing metropolis, an enormous melting pot fueled by waves of European immigration. Many of these immigrants, particularly Italians and Spaniards, settled in the port district, or *barrío*, of La Boca. It was a bustling working-class neighbourhood known for its vibrant culture, maritime industry, and strong community bonds. Football, introduced by British expatriates in the late 19th century, quickly became a popular pastime among locals. Numerous informal teams formed across the city, particularly in working-class districts where the sport provided an accessible source of entertainment and community identity.

Between the decade of 1900 and 1910, around three hundred football clubs were created in Argentina. An important one occurred on April 3, 1905. Some young men, the sons of Italian immigrants (specifically from Genoa) and La Boca residents, Esteban Baglietto, Alfredo Scarpati, Santiago Sana, and the brothers Teodoro and Juan Antonio Farenga had all gathered in Plaza Solís, a small square in the La Boca neighbourhood, to create a football club that would represent their community.

BAGLIETTO, SCARPATI and Sana were classmates in the Higher School of Commerce (now known as the Carlos Pellegrini High School of Commerce since 1908), then located on Bartolomé Mitre Street in central Buenos Aires. There they had, as a physical education teacher, an Irishman named Paddy MacCarthy, who was an ex-sailor from Cashel, Tipperary. He had also been a football player who instilled in his students the value of sport, while teaching them the techniques of boxing and, more pertinently, his beloved football.

On Monday, April 3rd, 1905, after their classes had finished, the young men had met in the home of Baglietto, on Ministro Brin Street in La Boca with the aim of creating a club dedicated to football. The boys, obviously excited at the prospect of creating such a club while the Bagliettos had visitors, caused such a commotion that Baglietto senior dismissed the boys from the modest house and from there they crossed the street and sat on a bench in Plaza

Solís, a small park in the eastern end of the *barrío*. It was here that Club Atlético Boca Juniors was formed.

One of the most crucial early decisions was the club's name. Some names were considered such as *Sons Of Italy*, *Defenders of La Boca* and *Stars of Italy*, before the founders settled on "Boca Juniors," a name that paid homage to their neighbourhood while also adding the English term "Juniors," reflecting the influence of British football culture which for many encapsulated prestige, commonplace at the time. They agreed that Baglietto, then just 18 years old, would serve as the club's first president. However, it was because of his young age that he was succeeded some days later by the Uruguayan Luis Cerezo as the club's president.

The newly formed Boca Juniors faced immediate challenges. They lacked a permanent playing ground, funding, and proper kits. In their early days, the team played friendly matches in various open fields around La Boca and the nearby Dársena Sud, sometimes using makeshift goalposts. However, their dedication and fighting spirit soon gained them recognition among local football enthusiasts.

Boca Juniors' inaugural football match took place on April 21, 1905, at Dársena Sud. In this historic encounter, Boca faced local side Mariano Moreno and secured a decisive 4–0 victory. The goals were scored by Juan Farenga with two goals, as well as José Farenga, and Santiago Sana. They wore black and white striped shirts for the game. Boca would wear a few shirts before adopting the final one, the famous blue with a wide horizontal yellow band.

On its official website, the club reports that there is an unverified version that states that the first shirt was pink and that it was used only in the first two games. However, it's generally agreed by most historians that, from day one, the team adopted a white shirt with black vertical stripes, which was made by the sister of the Farenga brothers, Manuela. They also briefly wore a light blue shirt before changing to a thinly striped dark navy and white shirt.

The colours of the club would become hugely important. Club president Juan Rafael Bricchetto proposed the now-famous colours at an assembly. He would later say that the colours were inspired from the flag of a ship at the city's port, where he worked. There are many myths as to which ship exactly gave Bricchetto the inspiration. The Swedish ship *Drottning Sophia* is often credited with this but, strictly speaking, it is impossible to know exactly which ship sailed into port that caught the club president's eye. Between the last days of 1906 and March 1907, several ships arrived in Buenos Aires sporting the flag of Sweden. The likeliest candidate, according to renowned Boca historian Sergio Lodise, is actually a ship called the *Oscar II*.

There is another lesser-known myth that the founders' physical education teacher, the Irishman, Paddy MacCarthy, had inspired them to use the colours of his native county of Tipperary GAA, an amateur sporting association in Ireland who play primarily gaelic football and hurling, whose shirts are, even to this day, identical to Boca's famous shirt. This myth most definitely isn't true.

Once Boca Juniors officially adopted their now-famous blue and yellow colours, the yellow band was initially diagonal before adopting a thick horizontal stripe. With their new identity, Boca Juniors began to gain recognition across Buenos Aires. Their reputation as a fierce, determined, and hardworking team increased with each match. They started competing more seriously in amateur leagues and tournaments, quickly climbing the ranks of Argentine football. The team's aggressive and passionate style of play resonated with their working-class supporters, fostering something of an immediate and deep connection between the club and its fans.

In 1913, Boca Juniors achieved their first major milestone by earning promotion to the Argentine First Division. This was a defining moment in the club's history, proving that they were ready to compete at the highest level. The blue and yellow colours became synonymous with success, passion, and the fighting spirit of La Boca.

Boca's rise was not without challenges. The club struggled to find a permanent home ground, often playing in different locations. However, their growing fan base and increasing influence in Argentine football motivated them to continue pushing forward. Boca was not just another team; it had become a symbol of pride for its supporters.

Boca had quickly found its rival in River Plate. Both teams had originated in La Boca. There are disputed dates with previous meetings between the two sides in unofficial matches going back to 1908, but the first league game between the rivals occurred in Racing Club's stadium, known then as Estadio Alsina y Colón in Avellaneda on August 24, 1913. River won the game 2-1. This fixture would later become one of the most intense and spectacular derbies in world football, known as the Superclásico.

Boca Juniors won their first league title in 1919, a landmark achievement that established them as a dominant force in Argentine football. The Argentine football league at the time was undergoing structural changes, with divisions between amateur and professional clubs creating a turbulent footballing landscape. The championship was organized by Asociación Argentina de Football (AAF). That year there was a split and another association was created, the Asociación Amateurs de Football, an unofficial dissident league which was for eight years without affiliation to FIFA. Boca always remained loyal to the official entity (AAF). Key players in the squad included Pedro Calomino, a highly skilled winger known for his dribbling and technical ability, and Alfredo Garasini, a dependable player who controlled the team's tempo on the field.

At this time, Boca had their own stadium at Ministro Brin y Senguel in La Boca. The stadium was constructed with a modest wooden structure, typical of the era, and had a limited capacity. However, it provided the club with a more stable home ground after years of playing in various fields around Buenos Aires.

The club had previously played at multiple locations, including Isla Demarchi in relatively nearby Puerto Madero and Wilde, a district named after Dr. José Wilde (a distant relative of one Irish writer named Oscar Wilde) which is several kilometres south of La Boca. The distance from the old neighbourhood meant that club membership dropped from 1,500 down to 300. The move to Wilde was supposed to be a temporary move, but the club knew that because of the membership drop, they would have to do what it takes to return to the old *barrío*. They finally returned to La Boca and settled at Ministro Brin y Senguel.

Following their triumph in 1919, Boca continued their dominance by winning their second league title in 1920. Once again competing in the league, the club finished the season at the top, showcasing consistency and strength. This back-to-back title run solidified Boca's place among Argentina's elite clubs.

By 1923, Boca secured their third league championship, further cementing their status as a powerhouse in Argentine football. This championship, followed by their unbeaten run the following year continued to enhance Boca's reputation, increasing their fanbase and solidifying their identity as a club that represented the working-class spirit combined with Italian traditions in La Boca. The previous year, the club had acquired a plot of land at the intersection of Brandsen and Del Crucero streets, a move that would lay the foundation for one of football's most legendary stadiums. This site is where La Bombonera stands today.

The decision to establish a stadium at Brandsen and Del Crucero was not without challenges. The club had to negotiate with Southern Railway, who owned the site, and secure financial backing to make the move possible. They relied heavily on the contributions of its members and supporters, many of whom played an active role in fundraising efforts.

The choice of location was also significant. Situated in the heart of La Boca, the new stadium site ensured that Boca would remain firmly rooted in its origins. Unlike rivals River Plate, which had now moved away from La Boca to far more affluent areas, Boca's commitment to staying in the neighbourhood further strengthened their connection with their slowly-growing fanbase and the stadium at Brandsen y Del Crucero.

While some of the most famous players in the sport's history are synonymous with the club, in the 1920's the club had an early idol in Américo Miguel Tesoriere. A legendary goalkeeper, Tesoriere was born in the *barrío* La Boca and played for the Xeneizes from 1917 until 1927, winning numerous silverware. Such was his presence, he was the first footballer to appear on the cover of Argentina's sports magazine *El Gráfico* in July 1922. Tesoriere would be one of many legendary players that would later be etched in stone of the club's history.

CHAPTER TWO

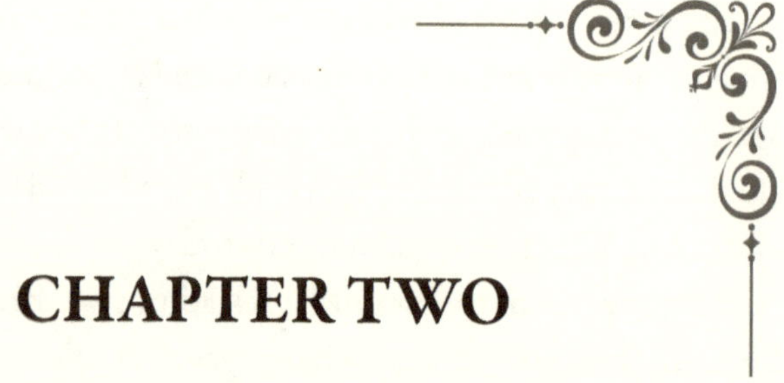

With their success on the pitch, an idea of sending a national team to tour in Europe in 1925 arose within AAF having witnessed the sensation generated by the Uruguayan football team in the 1924 Olympics in Paris, where they won a gold medal under the guidance of Ernesto Fígoli.

The national team idea fell through and having heard about the association's idea, Boca informed the Asociación Argentina de Football that they would undertake the tour. They were granted permission and allowed the club to postpone their league matches for 1925 if they would be the club to undertake the tour. Boca faced logistical challenges in organizing the tour. Travel arrangements had to be made, funds secured, and exhibition matches scheduled with various clubs across Spain, Germany, and France. The journey itself required a long transatlantic voyage, a grueling experience that tested the endurance of the players even before they had even set foot on European soil.

Finally, on February 4, 1925, the squad embarked for Europe aboard the ship *Formosa*, the squad was given an affectionate farewell from thousands of fans who gathered in the vicinity of the port. After twenty-two long days at sea, they arrived at their initial destination, Vigo.

Throughout the trip the team was accompanied by a Boca fan named Victoriano Caffarena, who financed part of the tour and was designated as a kit-man. He was affectionately known as player number 12, which has since been famously adopted by Boca fans to this day.

The motivation behind the tour was twofold. Firstly, it was an opportunity to showcase Argentine football talent to European audiences, many of whom were unfamiliar with the quality of South American football. Secondly, it provided Boca Juniors with the chance to measure themselves against Europe's elite clubs, gaining invaluable experience in international competition.

The first match of the tour was on March 5, 1925, against Celta Vigo, before 25,000 spectators in Campo de Coia. Such was the expectation in this game, that during the first half, the roof of a neighbouring factory where workers were standing upon watching the match had collapsed, causing two deaths and 26 injuries. For this reason the game was suspended for 16 minutes. Finally the game continued and Boca managed to win in their debut by 3-1. Three days later the game was replayed at the same venue in which Celta this time had won 3-1, two of the goals came from penalties.

BOCA ALSO FACED DEPORTIVO La Coruña, Real Madrid, Atlético Madrid, and a number of other top Spanish clubs including Espanyol, Osasuna, and Athletic Club. The Argentine team quickly earned respect for their technical ability, quick passing, and aggressive attacking style. Despite playing against well-established Spanish clubs, Boca Juniors held their own winning 10 out of 13 games in Spain, drawing praise from Spanish football press.

Following their successful stint in Spain, Boca traveled to Germany, where they faced stiffer competition from clubs such as Bayern Munich and Eintracht Frankfurt. German football, known for its physicality and tactical discipline, posed a different challenge for the *el Xeneize*, but they adapted quickly, demonstrating versatility in their playstyle. The matches in Germany were crucial in preparing the team for future international competitions, as they were exposed to a variety of playing styles and strategies. They left this leg of the tour unbeaten.

The final leg of the tour took Boca to France for their sole game in Paris. They took the Stade Bergeyre on June 7th, 1925, where they faced a combined Paris XI, composed of the best players from the local clubs and Boca won the match 4-2. By the time they concluded their European journey, the Argentine club had played 19 matches, winning 15, drawing 1, and losing 3—an impressive record that showcased their dominance.

The 1925 European tour had a profound impact on Boca Juniors and Argentine football as a whole. Firstly, it elevated Boca's status as an international club who are easily capable of competing with Europe's elite teams. The success of the tour solidified Boca's position as Argentina's premier football club and contributed to the rising popularity of the sport in the country.

Furthermore, the tour helped Argentine football gain recognition on the global stage. Prior to Boca's European adventure, South American teams were often underestimated by their European counterparts. Boca's strong performances forced European clubs to acknowledge the high level of skill and competitiveness present in Argentine football.

Upon their return to Buenos Aires, Boca Juniors were met with a hero's welcome. Thousands of supporters gathered at the port to greet their triumphant team, celebrating what was regarded as a monumental achievement in the club's history. AAF had awarded Boca with an honorary title in recognition of their success in Europe. They had also minted gold medals for the squad. The 1925 European tour remains one of the most significant milestones in Boca's history. The club had now gained enormous acclaim from fans and the media throughout the country, and were recognised as a force of Argentine football. Now football fans from different neighbourhoods, and even different parts of the country, were very interested to see what this team from La Boca can do.

The 1930s were a transformative decade for the club, marked by their transition from amateur to professional football, major successes in domestic competitions, and significant developments in club infrastructure. During this period, Boca further cemented its reputation as one of Argentina's most dominant and popular teams, while their home at Brandsen y Del Crucero became the epicentre of their passionate and ever-growing fanbase.

One of the most significant moments in Boca Juniors' history came in 1931 when Argentine football officially turned professional. Boca embraced the change seamlessly, winning the inaugural professional league title that same year. To make things even sweeter for *el Xeneize*, they beat bitter rivals River Plate 3-0 in the final fixture of the season.

With key players such as Francisco Varallo, Roberto Cherro, and Delfín Benítez Cáceres, Boca dominated the competition. The club finished the 1931 season with 50 points, securing the title ahead of San Lorenzo and River Plate. This championship victory solidified significantly increased the number of supporters attending matches at Brandsen y Del Crucero.

It was during this year that the Board of Directors, headed by President Ruperto Molfino, decided to purchase 21,471 m² of the land where the stadium was situated, for two million pesos, an enormous sum of money. It was time to make a far greater arena.

While other teams sought out new locations for larger, more modern stadiums, Boca refused to leave La Boca. The club had grown within these streets, and to abandon the neighbourhood would have meant abandoning its very identity. River Plate had done just that, moving north to Núñez and building El Monumental, a colossal stadium that was widely regarded as the most modern football venue in Argentina. Boca, however, had no intention of following that path. Instead, the club would build something even greater, something more unique, something that could stand in defiance of the forces that had driven other teams away from their roots. And so, the decision was made: Boca Juniors would construct a new stadium, not elsewhere, but on the same sacred ground they had called home for years.

On February 18th, 1938, under the presidency of Dr Camilo Cichero, the cornerstone was laid in the presence of the nation's President Agustín Pedro Justo. Boca last played in its wooden stadium on April 10th, 1938 in a game against River, who won the tie 2-1.

The challenge, however, was immense. The land available was limited, hemmed in by the narrow streets of the neighbourhood and the ever-expanding city of Buenos Aires around it. A conventional stadium design simply would not work. If Boca was to build a stadium worthy of its stature, it would have to be something revolutionary.

Enter Slovenian architect Viktor Sulčič and local engineer José Luis Delpini, as well as geometer Raúl Bes, who would change the club forever. The solution they devised was as bold as it was quite unprecedented. Rather than build outwards, they would build upwards. Instead of sprawling stands, they would construct towering walls of concrete, rising almost vertically, bringing the fans as close to the action as possible, while creating an intimidating atmosphere for visiting teams.

From the moment construction began, the stadium became a labor of love for the Boca community. Clubs were backed financially by its members. While financing the construction of a stadium based solely on membership would have been impossible, Boca, like many clubs, sought help from the government in the form of long-term loans to keep the dream alive.

The fans rallied behind the project, donating money, buying special bonds issued by the club, and offering whatever support they could. This was not just the construction of a stadium; it was a communal effort, a statement of defiance, a declaration that el Xeneize would remain where they belonged.

On Saturday, May 25th, 1940 the Estadio Boca Juniors was inaugurated. President Cichero cut the blue and yellow ribbons to officially open the stadium. Then a parade took place, which featured former players and figures from the club's 35 year history. But sad news lingered in the new arena, that one of the club's very first board of directors and former president Juan Rafael Bricchetto had passed away two days prior.

The opening match, a friendly against San Lorenzo, was a spectacle, drawing thousands of Boca supporters eager to experience the new sporting cathedral of La Boca. As the first goal was scored, as the stands erupted in celebration, as the walls shook with the deafening roar of the fans, it was evident that something extraordinary had been created.

The stadium at this point had no floodlights and the southern hemisphere's sunset would usually occur around 5.30pm and so with that it was agreed that the game would last 70 minutes, playing simply 35 minutes for each half. Boca won the game 2-0. The neighbourhood, and the fans, were overjoyed with not just the result, but with this incredible stadium. It was, and still is, a colossus that stood out within La Boca's narrow streets. There is now a new temple for which Boca fans can worship.

Boca Juniors entered the 1940s with a squad poised for greatness. After a strong finish to the previous decade, the club, under the management of Alfredo Garassini, set its sights on reclaiming domestic supremacy. The year 1940 would prove to be momentous, not just for the silverware the club would earn, but for the landmark that would change its future forever: the opening of La Bombonera.

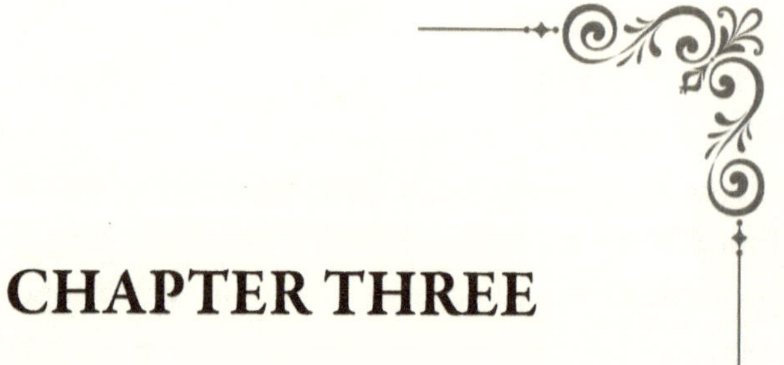

CHAPTER THREE

The team of 1940 was built around a solid defensive line and a dynamic attack led by Jaime Sarlanga, the prolific forward whose name would be etched into Boca's history books. Alongside players like Bernardo Gandulla and Mario Boyé, Boca stormed through the Primera División season, clinching the title with a decisive 5-2 victory over Independiente. It was a triumph that set the tone for the decade—the Xeneize was here to dominate.

The early years of the 1940s, World War Two had broken out in Europe, but Boca had asserted itself as a national powerhouse with La Bombonera encapsulating their grand scale. The first modification in the stadium took place on November 16, 1941, where an extension was added to the north end of the stadium (where La 12 currently stands), later named after Boca idol Natalio Pescia, a one-club-man who played for the club from 1942 until 1956.

IT WAS THE CONSECUTIVE league titles of 1943 and 1944 that further cemented its reputation. The 1943 campaign was particularly memorable, with Boca showcasing attacking brilliance and defensive grit.

That season, Jaime Sarlanga once again stood out, finishing as the club's top scorer. Boca's midfield was marshaled by the brilliant Ernesto Lazzatti, known as *the golden kid*, a player known for his intelligence on the ball and leadership qualities. Lazzatti, alongside Carlos Sosa and Natalio Pescia, formed a midfield trio that dictated Boca's play. The team's unwavering consistency saw them claim the title, fending off a strong challenge from River Plate.

The following year, Boca defended its crown with another impressive campaign. The title was secured in emphatic fashion with a 3-0 victory over Racing Club in the final fixture. The match, played at River Plate's stadium due to La Bombonera undergoing maintenance, saw Boca's attacking force dismantle Racing with clinical precision.

That 1944 squad was one of Boca's finest: Claudio Vacca in goal, the defensive pairing of Marante and Valussi, and an attacking trident featuring Sarlanga, Boyé, and Corcuera. More significantly, Boca set a professional-era record by remaining unbeaten for 26 consecutive matches, a testament to their tactical discipline and sheer determination.

The 1940s also saw the Boca-River rivalry reach new levels of intensity. The "Superclásico" was always a heated affair, but with both clubs emerging as the dominant forces of the decade, the matches became battles of pride, passion, and prestige.

In 1945, Boca recorded one of its most famous victories against River Plate, crushing their arch-rivals 4-1 in front of a packed La Bombonera. The match remains legendary, not just for the score-line, but for the manner in which Boca dismantled a River side that included some of the biggest stars of the time, such as Adolfo Pedernera and Angel Labruna.

Throughout the decade, the rivalry was evenly contested, with both clubs sharing league titles. River's "La Máquina" side, a team known for its fluid attacking play, provided stern opposition, but Boca's grit and determination ensured they remained a thorn in River's side. Every Superclásico during this era was a spectacle, an event that captivated Buenos Aires and divided the city along fiercely loyal lines.

By the 1940s, Boca's fanbase had become the most passionate in Argentina. The club's humble roots attracted supporters from all over Buenos Aires, particularly from the port districts. These were fans who saw Boca as more than just a football club—it was a symbol of their struggles, their triumphs, and their identity.

Matchdays at La Bombonera were unlike any other. Thousands of blue and yellow-clad supporters would march through the streets, filling the air with songs, chants, and an unmatched energy. The Boca-River divide wasn't just about football; it reflected social and economic differences as well. Boca represented the working-class immigrants of Buenos Aires, while River was associated with the more affluent neighbourhoods, earning them the nickname "Los Millonarios", a nickname they still use today.

As Buenos Aires itself underwent changes, with rapid industrialization and an enormous influx of European immigrants reshaping its identity, Boca Juniors remained a constant—a club that embodied the soul of the people. Football, more than ever, was intertwined with everyday life, and the Xeneize was absolutely at the heart of it all.

The year 1946 was a pivotal one, not just for Boca Juniors, but for Argentina as a whole. The end of wartime brought significant shifts in global politics and economics, and Argentina, under the newly elected president Juan Domingo Perón, was entering an era of social and economic transformation. Perón's rise to power marked the beginning of a movement that would shape Argentine society for decades to come, and football—particularly Boca Juniors—was deeply intertwined with these changes.

While Boca did not secure the league title in 1946, they remained competitive throughout the season, with Mario Boyé continuing to shine as one of the country's most prolific forwards. That year, Boca finished third in the Primera División, behind champions San Lorenzo and runners-up, rivals River Plate.

Perón's presidency had a direct impact on football, as his government recognized the sport's cultural significance. He sought to use football as a unifying force, pouring state resources into the game and ensuring that working-class Argentines—many of whom were Boca supporters—could enjoy matches at an affordable price.

It is said that Perón himself was a Racing fan, this however was not true. The truth was he wasn't as interested in football, as its fans were. His preferred sport was fencing.

Meanwhile, Buenos Aires itself was undergoing rapid industrialization, bringing even more working-class immigrants into the city. This urban shift further strengthened Boca's identity as the club of the people. The atmosphere at La Bombonera in 1946 was electric, as thousands packed the stadium week after week, chanting passionately and reinforcing the stadium's reputation as one of the most intimidating venues in world football.

CHAPTER FOUR

In 1950, Boca's leadership, led by then-president Daniel José Gil, recognized the urgent need to increase the stadium's capacity. La Bombonera, originally built in 1940, had already become too small for Boca's ever-growing fanbase. Matches were consistently sold out, with thousands of supporters unable to secure entry, leading to growing frustrations and logistical challenges on matchdays.

Discussions for expansion began in earnest in late 1950, with initial blueprints being drafted in early 1951. The club sought approval from the Buenos Aires municipal government to proceed with the development. The approval process was not without its hurdles, as concerns about construction feasibility and neighbourhood impact were raised. However, by mid-1952, while the entire nation was mourning the loss of Eva Peron, Boca brought their fans some joy by having secured the necessary permits, so construction was set to begin.

The expansion project officially broke ground in September 1952. The third tier was to be built on the east side of the stadium, following the same steep vertical design that had made La Bombonera unique. The club worked with engineer Viktor Sulčič, who had played a crucial role in the stadium's initial construction. He also ensured that, even though Buenos Aires is not in a seismic region, even if there was an earthquake then La Bombonera would remain intact. An interesting and little known fact is that the third tier was named Juan Domingo Perón, and has never been changed.

THE LOGISTICAL CHALLENGES of the project were immense. The stadium's location in the densely populated La Boca neighbourhood meant that expansion had to be carefully managed to avoid disrupting daily life. Construction was carried out in phases to ensure that Boca Juniors could continue playing matches at home throughout the process. Despite material shortages—due in part to Argentina's fluctuating economy—the project remained on schedule.

On April 5, 1953, the third tier was completed along with the much-needed floodlighting. The decision to expand was made almost four years prior after demand grew, and the need for lighting was vital so matches could be played after fans finished work. Boca marked the occasion by staging a friendly match against Yugoslav side Hajduk Split which finished at 1-1, with the final whistle coming at almost midnight. The newly expanded stadium could now officially hold over 57,000 spectators, making it now one of the largest football venues in South America. Combined with the flood lighting system also meant that the ground was now considered with the elite stadiums at the time.

The first official match played with the newly expanded stadium took place on April 19, 1953. Boca Juniors faced Newell's Old Boys in front of a record-breaking crowd. The new tier's impact was immediately felt, with the stands reverberating with even greater intensity than before. The game ended in a thrilling 3-2 victory for Boca, with star forward José Borello scoring twice to mark the occasion.

The stadium's new look was celebrated across the city, and indeed the country, with media outlets praising Boca's ambitious expansion. Fans embraced the change wholeheartedly, with chants and songs celebrating "La Bombonera más grande" (The bigger Bombonera) becoming part of Boca's matchday culture.

The financial boost provided by the expansion allowed Boca Juniors to strengthen its squad significantly in the following years. Key signings in the mid-1950s helped the club regain its dominance in Argentine football, culminating in a league title in 1954.

The late 1950's was a critical era in the history of Boca, a time when the club navigated through both triumphs and tribulations on the pitch while also experiencing significant cultural and social shifts off the field. It was an era defined by economic instability in Argentina, political turbulence, and changing dynamics within Buenos Aires, all of which impacted the trajectory of the club. Throughout these years, the club remained a powerful entity in Argentine football, competing fiercely in the domestic league and fostering an even deeper connection with its fans, who saw Boca as a representation of their struggles, passions, and identity.

By 1955, the club was still basking in the glow of its early 1950s success. Having won the league title in 1954, the club was eager to maintain its dominance in the domestic league. However, the team faced a strong challenge from fierce rivals River Plate, as well as rising teams like Independiente and Racing Club, both of whom were making their mark in Argentine football. The league was becoming increasingly competitive, and Boca found itself battling fiercely in the top half of the standings year after year.

One of the defining characteristics of Boca during this period was the club's ability to maintain a passionate fanbase despite inconsistent performances. The team fell short of winning the Primera División titles in the late 1950s, often finishing in the top three but failing to secure the ultimate prize. The disappointment among fans was palpable, but their loyalty never wavered. The home matches at La Bombonera continued to quickly sell out, with the stadium pulsating with the energy of thousands of loyal Xeneize fans. This period solidified Boca's identity as a club that, even in moments of adversity, could rely on an unparalleled level of devotion from its fanbase.

Off the pitch, Boca was undergoing significant changes. The club administration sought to modernize various aspects of its operations, improving facilities and youth development programs. The recent expansion of La Bombonera, allowed Boca to accommodate even more fans, making it one of the most intimidating stadiums in South America. Additionally, the club was beginning to recognize the importance of commercial partnerships and sponsorships, an aspect of football that was becoming more prominent worldwide. While Boca remained deeply tied to its working-class roots, there was an awareness that financial stability was essential for continued success.

The late 1950s also saw Argentina grappling with economic and political challenges that had direct implications for football clubs. The overthrow of President Juan Domingo Perón in 1955 marked a major turning point in Argentine history. Perón had been a strong advocate for the working class and had championed policies that benefited football clubs, particularly those with deep connections to the people, like many fans of Boca. The policies of Perón were largely directed at expanding the appeal and strengthening the infrastructure of sport, and football became a main priority. Perón was eager to project a positive image of his country as political propaganda. Perón was immensely popular with many, but certainly not all, the Xeneize fans, who often chanted "Boca y Perón, una solo corazon". Perón saw the potential for harnessing the positive energies of sport for furthering an image of national pride and unity. He coined slogans such as "Perón, The First Sportsman" and "Perón Sponsors Sports" to strengthen his image as a leader for football fans nationwide. His removal from power led to economic fluctuations and social unrest, affecting ticket sales, player salaries, and overall club operations. Boca, like many Argentine clubs, had to navigate through these uncertain times while maintaining its standing as a footballing institution.

CHAPTER FIVE

Despite the off-the-field challenges, Boca continued to fight for supremacy in the Argentine league. In 1959, after a 13-year drought, San Lorenzo were the team who won the championship, with Boca finishing in 8th. The highlights of 1959 included the double victory over rivals River; a 5-1 thrashing in La Bombonera and overcoming a 2-0 deficit to defeat a deflated Los Millionarios side 2-3.

Another key development around this time was Boca's increasing participation in international competitions. The emergence of South American club tournaments meant that Boca now had the opportunity to test itself against teams from Brazil, Uruguay, and beyond. Although these competitions were still in their infancy, Boca's presence in such tournaments further solidified its status as a club with continental aspirations. Facing South American giants like Peñarol and Santos provided invaluable experience for the team.

The 1960 season marked the beginning of another transitional phase for Boca. The club continued to invest in new talent, with a focus on blending experienced players with promising youngsters. The goal was to build a squad that could reclaim domestic glory while also making a mark internationally.

A crucial turning point for the club came that year with the return of Alberto Armando as club president. Armando had previously served as Boca's president from 1954 until 1955, but his return marked the beginning of a new era of ambition and modernization for the club. Recognizing the changing landscape of Argentine football, Armando sought to expand Boca's influence both domestically and internationally. He prioritized infrastructure improvements, player acquisitions, and financial stability.

Throughout Buenos Aires, Boca remained an essential part of the city's cultural fabric. The club's matches were more than just football games; they were social events that brought communities together. The working-class neighbourhoods of La Boca and beyond identified deeply with the team, seeing in Boca a reflection of their own struggles and triumphs. The songs and chants of Boca supporters became anthems of resilience, echoing through the streets long after matches had ended. Football was not just a sport—it was a way of life, and Boca was at its core.

By the time 1961 arrived, Boca was poised for yet another push toward the top. While league titles had proven elusive in the latter half of the 1950s, the club remained an undeniable powerhouse, continuously competing at the highest level. The infrastructure improvements made in previous years, the continued support of its boisterous and brilliant fanbase, and the integration of new footballing philosophies all suggested that Boca's best years may well be yet to come.

In the early 1960's, while most of the world, for better or worse, was experiencing change to the sound of Beatlemania, the city of Buenos Aires was in transition. The tango, which once dictated the rhythm of the streets, now fought for space with the emerging pulse of modernization. The *subte* (the city's underground railway network) transported the ever expanding population around the capital. The grand avenues, from Avenida 9 de Julio to Corrientes, teemed with the movement of an evolving metropolis, its people caught between nostalgia and the need for something new. In La Boca, where the docks echoed with the voices of working men and the smell of grilled meat from the parrillas spilled into the streets, Boca remained the heart of it all.

A decisive moment came on December 9, 1962, when Boca faced River at La Bombonera. With the stadium packed to capacity, and the title race coming close to its conclusion between the two bitter rivals, Boca were 1-0 ahead when River were awarded a penalty with just six minutes to go. Brazilian striker Delem stepped up, and missed courtesy of Boca's legendary goalkeeper Antonio Roma. Jubilation in La Bombonera as el Xeneize held on for a famous victory. In the next round of games, a week later Boca were to face Estudiantes at home. A victory meant the title would go to the blue and yellow outfit. Boca dismantled their opponents in a stunning 4-0 victory, winning the Primera División for the first time in eight years, with rivals River Plate finishing runners up. The celebrations spilled out from the stands into the streets of La Boca, where fireworks crackled in the night sky and fans paraded through Almirante Brown, singing and weeping in joy. The beers were flowing as the sound was deafening. The neighbourhood had not seen anything like it in years. This was more than a title; this was a statement. Boca was back.

FRESH FROM THEIR DOMESTIC triumph, Boca set their sights on the continent. The Copa Libertadores, a competition still in its infancy, had fast become the ultimate prize, the battleground where clubs from across South America fought for supremacy. In 1963, Boca entered the tournament with a squad eager to prove itself. The group stage saw them go toe-to-toe with Olimpia, and Universidad de Chile in the group stage. Boca topped the group, with three wins out of four.

The next phase was a two-legged affair against Uruguayan side Peñarol. Having dramatically won the first leg in Montevideo in the final few minutes, the game at La Bombonera became the stuff of legend. On May 5, with the stadium at its absolute limit, possibly oversold and beyond its capacity, Boca secured a dramatic 1-0 victory with the game's only goal from serial goalscorer José Sanfilippo. At the final whistle, the stadium was shaking the concrete foundations as the fans roared in approval. The dream of continental glory edged closer.

But then came Santos. Pele's Santos. The Brazilian maestro was a household name throughout the world and it was around this time when he was considered by many to be truly at his peak. The Santos team was full of stars. World Cup winners such as Coutinho, Gilmar, Mauro Ramos and Zito joined Pele in Santos' starting XI. That is what stood between Boca and immortality.

The first leg of the final, played at the famous Maracanã on September 4, was a brutal encounter. Boca fought bravely, but Santos edged them out, 3-2. The return leg at La Bombonera, played before a crowd that yet again seemed to defy the laws of space, was meant to be the moment Boca overturned history. But Pele and Coutinho had other plans. Despite the relentless pressure from the stands, Santos claimed a 2-1 victory, and with it, the Copa Libertadores. For Boca, it was heartbreak. They had come so close, only to watch greatness slip through their fingers. But the fire had been lit. Boca would not rest until they held that trophy.

The following year, goalkeeper Antonio Roma went 742 minutes without conceding a goal. This was instrumental to Boca's 1964 league campaign. They may have only scored 35 goals all season, but it was their lack of conceding that definitely helped the club win the games that was crucial to their Premier División title. They finished the season six points clear of runners up Independiente. And the celebrations began with singing and dancing, the beer and wine were flowing with the ambience of fireworks and the fragrance of barbecued meats through the narrow streets of La Boca once more. This is Boca.

There was another relatively forgotten triumph that same year. In the middle of the season, the club received an invite to participate in an unlikely setting—Morocco, competing in the Mohammed V Cup, a tournament that would momentarily shift their focus from Buenos Aires to the exotic landscapes of North Africa.

The Mohammed V Cup, named in honour of the late Moroccan king, was a relatively new, yet somewhat prestigious international club tournament, with the 1964 edition held in Meknes, a small city around two and a half hours east of Casablanca. Upon arrival in Casablanca, the team was met with great fanfare. Moroccan football fans, many of whom were more than aware of this seemingly exotic team from South America, welcomed Boca with open arms, eager to see them compete against some of the world's best. It was a four team tournament; Boca were in with local champions RFA Rabat, French champions Saint-Étienne as well as Spanish giants Real Madrid.

Boca's first game was a 3-0 thrashing over Saint-Étienne, and their second game just two days later was the final against Real Madrid, led by the incredible Ferenc Puskás. On paper, Boca were the underdogs, but they relished the challenge. From the kick-off, Boca disrupted Madrid's rhythm with intense pressing and aggressive marking. An early goal from Ángel Clemente Rojas put Boca up 1-0, before the ever-reliable Puskás brought it back on level terms within five minutes. As the match wore on, Boca grew in confidence. The Moroccan crowd, most of whom were there to see a Madrid win, couldn't help but be enamoured by the Argentinean side's spirit. Then in the 74th minute, Rojas claimed another goal. The Xeneize held on for the victory, and the Spanish press were astounded that the mighty Real Madrid took a beating from this team from Buenos Aires. Though the Mohammed V Cup has since faded into football history, for Boca, it remains something of a cherished memory.

The following year was even more memorable for the club. Boca won their third championship in four years, topping the group by a point over bitter rivals River Plate in what seemed to be an ongoing occurrence in the 60's between the clubs; Boca first, River second. They won the league on the final day of the season following a 3-1 win against Club Atlético Atlanta in La Bombonera. Another party into the night around La Boca? Naturally.

By this point people weren't just coming from all over Buenos Aires to visit La Bombonera to watch Boca. They were making long journeys from all over Argentina. Uruguayans were taking the ferry from Montevideo, across the Rio de la Plata, to see this mythical cauldron of noise and passion.

Around this time, club president Alberto Armando lobbied the idea of moving Boca from La Bombonera. The president's first plan for an all-new stadium was a few years prior in 1960, at the grounds of the Casa Amarilla, just beside where the stadium sits today. But he was unable to realise this dream for various reasons. It was the engineer José Luis Delpini who suggested moving the idea to beside the river. With that, a few kilometres the the north-east by the Río de la Plata, close to Puerto Madero and at the south end of Avenida España, Armando found where he could Boca could potentially call home. The project was initially called *Area Costanera Sur*, until it was given the far more prestigious sounding name of *Ciudad Deportiva de Boca* (Boca Juniors Sports City). It was to include a 140,000 gigantic stadium, an enormous sports complex, various athletic venues, an aquarium, mini-golf courses, swimming pools among other attractions including a drive-in movie theatre that would hold 500 cars. National congress passed a law donating 40 hectares of reclaimed land from the river to the club for the construction of the new complex. Buenos Aires city officials emphasized the need for zones of recreation. The city and national government not only donated the land, but also promised to construct surface streets, dig underground tunnels, and link two major city thoroughfares to provide easy access to the Ciudad Deportiva.

NATIONAL LEADERS AND urban planners were prompted, largely by the city's wealthy voting middle class, to reshape downtown Buenos Aires and surrounding neighbourhoods as something of a modern world city built around capitalism, leisure and consumption. Since the early 1950s, the working class had been increasingly falling on harder times. Liveable wages for industrial workers declined throughout the late 1950s and inflation had reached 25%. Social divide between the city's working class and the military government was due to the former feeling somewhat invisible. Many of those who fell on hard times were pushed to the outskirts of Buenos Aires, with the south and west rapidly expanding. As a result, city planners were increasingly attentive to the patterns of consumption and recreation of the middle class in more affluent areas. Therefore it was only obvious that the Ciudad Deportiva was to be accessible from downtown areas rather than way out in the suburbs.

On Sunday 3rd of September 1965, Boca had begun filling the river and, within two years, had built several man-made islands, laid electrical works, and built two access bridges. By the following year, the club began selling bonds to the club's own members (*socios*) as well as investors and surpassed their own expectations by raising nearly two million pesos. In 1967, the bonds had raised three million pesos and just twelve months on, the figure rose to an incredible five million. The new stadium was to impressively double the capacity of bitter rival River Plate's Monumental, themselves already situated in an affluent part of Buenos Aires. The scale and ambition of constructing such an enormous stadium on a man-made island was unprecedented. It was to be located over a kilometre out from the coast and interestingly ignored some studies that showed that the whole complex could actually sink into the Río de la Plata.

Despite the huge costs and the ignored risks, everything except for the final island had been formed by 1971. In the six years since construction began, over half a million trucks had couriered millions of cubic metres of earth. Club president Armando offered a monthly raffle to truck drivers who hauled earth to win a brand new truck. Tennis courts, the aquarium, mini-golf courses, swimming pools were all opened to the public in phases between by the late '60's. But no sign of the grand stadium. In 1971 the club began the first phase constructing Boca's new home ground with Armando promising to have it built three years ahead of the plan to showcase it to the world in the opening match of the 1978 World Cup, as well as the final. There was even an inauguration date, May 25th, 1975, that was advertised in newspapers and local magazines.

Sadly the project was rife with problems and increasing debts. Costs for the stadium had risen almost three times in 1973 alone. Financing for the project simply dried up. Armando also lost significant government support when Perón returned to the presidency in 1973. The club's president had backed the candidate running against Perón's candidate in the 1973 elections. In addition to this, there were certain people within the club that accused Armando of mismanaging the funds. The Ciudad Deportiva showed an effort by Boca to increase their revenue and announce themselves as an elite club to the entire world. But in doing so, they would be attracting the middle class, therefore it would not be representative of the club's roots - the working class in La Boca. For the vast majority, the fact that Boca still remains to this day in the same *barrio*, fuels extra passion into el Xeneize.

During the construction, one of the darkest moments in Argentine football history occurred. It was on the cold afternoon of Sunday, June 23, 1968, during a Superclásico between River Plate and Boca at the Monumental. At the end of the match, which ended in a 0-0 draw, a deadly human crush occurred at Gate 12, resulting in the deaths of 71 fans (though there are reports that claim this figure is even higher), most of them young with an average age of just 19. There were also more than 150 injured. Survivors reported chaotic scenes, with people falling on top of each other, suffocating in the crush. Some said they saw police batons striking the crowd, while others described a mass of bodies piling up against the closed gate. It was like a scene from an apocalyptic nightmare. Despite investigations, or perhaps the lack of, no one was ever officially held responsible for the disaster. The lack of clear findings and accountability has made the tragedy even more painful for the victims' families. This tragedy, known as the *tragedia de la puerta 12*, remains the worst stadium disaster in Argentine sporting history.

By the mid-1970s, Buenos Aires stood at a crossroads of political effervescence and political unrest. The city's European-style architecture bore witness to a society grappling with profound transformations. The death of President Perón in July 1974 had plunged the nation into uncertainty. His widow and successor, Isabel Perón, grappled with mounting unrest. The period saw the rise of what would be known as the "Dirty War," a campaign marked by state terrorism against suspected dissidents.

The year 1974 was pivotal for Boca. The team commenced the Torneo Metropolitano under the guidance of manager Rogelio Domínguez. Despite a squad brimming with talent, including the prolific striker Osvaldo Potente, who netted 20 goals that season, the results were inconsistent. Their campaign culminated in a third-place finish, with 12 wins, 3 draws, and 7 losses, tallying 43 goals for and 26 against.

A highlight of the season was the emphatic 5-2 victory over arch-rivals River Plate on February 3rd in a fiercely competitive match at La Bombonera. Debutant, 25-year-old Carlos García Cambón, made history by scoring four goals, a record in Superclásico debuts.

By the time 1976 had come around, it was not to be merely another campaign in the storied history of the club; it was in fact a turning point that encapsulated the spirit of a nation grappling with political upheaval, societal transformation, and the enduring love for the beautiful game. Amid the backdrop of a turbulent political climate following the military coup in March of that year, Boca found itself at a crossroads—a crucible in which on-field brilliance and off-field pressures merged into a narrative of defiance, unity, and passionate ambition.

The season unfolded during one of Argentina's most challenging periods, when the country's social and political fabric was being rewoven by forces both internal and external. The new military regime sought to reshape every aspect of public life, including the world of sports. Football, a cornerstone of Argentine identity, was no exception. Authorities recognized the potent influence of clubs like Boca in molding public sentiment and employed the medium to disseminate a narrative of national pride and resilience. In this charged atmosphere, Boca's matches were more than contests of skill and strategy; they became symbolic battlegrounds where the fervor of the fans intersected with the aspirations of a people yearning for hope and identity.

On the pitch, the evolution of Boca's playing style was evident. The team's approach blended disciplined defensive organization with a daring, free-flowing attack that captivated spectators. The defensive line—anchored by players whose physical presence and tactical intelligence were second to none—formed a formidable barrier against opposing offenses. Their ability to read the game and intercept passes was complemented by a midfield that boasted creative dynamism. This group, a mix of experienced veterans and promising young talents, became the engine of the team, orchestrating intricate passing sequences that often left opponents scrambling. Their vision and technical skills allowed them to exploit gaps in enemy formations, setting the stage for rapid counter-attacks that frequently caught defences off guard.

CHAPTER SIX

One of the greatest Superclásico moments occurred on Wednesday 22nd of December, 1976. It was the final of the Nacional Championship and the atmosphere was electrifying—a reminder that in Argentina, football was more than a game; it was a way of life. The rivalry between the two clubs was already intense, but this match carried an unprecedented weight—it was a direct battle for a major title.

It has been said that prior to kick-off, referee Arturo Ithurralde went to the dressing rooms to inform the captains of a new regulation: a free kick could be taken whenever the player wished, provided that no wall had been requested.

Boca, led by Juan Carlos Lorenzo, was a rugged, defensive, yet highly tactical team, while River, under Ángel Labruna, was a slightly more technical and attacking squad. Both clubs had strong lineups, with Boca featuring legends like Hugo Gatti, Francisco Sá, Juan Taverna, and Ruben Suñé, while River had stars such as Ubaldo Fillol, Daniel Passarella, and Oscar Mas. Tensions ran high on the pitch, and both teams played aggressively, knowing that one goal could decide everything. And one goal did. In the 72nd minute, Daniel Passarella fouled Carlos 'Toti' Veglio just outside the River area, and Ruben Suñé, who was in his debut season with Boca having joined from Unión de Santa Fe, recalled what he'd learned in the dressing room from the referee. Goalkeeper Pato Fillol was setting up a wall when the Boca midfielder called out to referee Ithurralde, saying "I'll shoot," before the ball crashed into the corner. The referee had no choice but to award the goal, which proved decisive. Boca ended up winning that historic final 1-0 thanks to the quick thinking of their captain. The River players furiously protested, arguing that they had not been given time to organize their defence. The River fans in the terrace were going absolutely crazy. But the referee stood by his decision.

THE FOOTAGE OF THE winning goal became known as *El Gol Fantasma* ("The Ghost Goal"). It seemed to have been erased from history. The game was indeed televised, but few got to see the actual goal. The reasons are somewhat unclear, but it has been said that it is because the leaders of Argentina's military leadership that ran the country under a dictatorship at the time, most notably Jorge Rafael Videla, Emilio Eduardo Massera and Orlando Ramón Agosti, held strong allegiances to River Plate with some of them allegedly being named as honorary members. They were allegedly the ones who ordered the footage to be removed from history. They wanted this embarrassment taken from people's televisions and from their memories. In reality, this wasn't really the case. It was simply that the country wasn't great at preserving its history in those days, and merely taped over the footage.

The following year stands as a watershed moment in the storied history of Boca Juniors. The season unfolded under the weight of considerable expectation. Fans, steeped in tradition and fueled by a deep sense of belonging, filled the streets of La Boca, and the stands of La Bombonera with a passion that bordered on the religious. Every match became an event of national significance, a moment to assert identity in the face of socio-political challenges. For the players and the management alike, 1977 was a call to reimagine the very nature of football, blending time-honoured values with innovative tactics that would not only elevate the team's status in Argentina but also leave an indelible mark on the global game. It was a year when every pass, every tackle, and every goal was laden with meaning—a living, breathing testimony to the club's enduring spirit. With an emphasis on technical skill and tactical ingenuity, Boca set out to transform adversity into artistic expression on the pitch.

The pulse of Argentina beat fiercely under a sky heavy with expectation and uncertainty, Boca embarked on a quest that would etch their name into the annals of football history—the Copa Libertadores. For Boca, a club with deep roots in the working-class neighbourhood La Boca, and with an identity forged through decades of triumph and tribulation, the Libertadores was not merely an international tournament; it was a proving ground where passion, strategy, and collective spirit converged. From the moment the draw was announced, there was an unspoken promise among the players, staff, and fans that this campaign would be different—a campaign defined by a relentless hunger for glory and a desire to vindicate years of domestic success on the continental stage.

In the corridors of La Bombonera, where every brick and every chant resonated with the dreams of countless supporters, the Copa Libertadores was seen as the ultimate challenge. The weight of expectation was enormous, yet it was met with a sense of purpose and an unwavering commitment to the club's storied traditions. Every training session, every tactical discussion, and every whispered word of encouragement in the changing room was imbued with the knowledge that the Libertadores was a chance to demonstrate that Boca was not just a local institution but a continental—perhaps even a global beacon of footballing excellence. Coaches and players alike were acutely aware of the historic significance of the tournament; it was a stage where the best teams from South America converged, and the opportunity to overcome them promised not only silverware but also a lasting legacy.

In 1977, while punk rock was taking Europe and the USA by a significant cultural storm, Argentina was a nation in difficult circumstances, its people under a regime that suppressed. But it was indeed the people who celebrated the beauty of football. For *bosteros*, each matchday in La Bombonera was an escape for them, and Boca as a gigantic footballing institution embodied the struggle, bravery, and unyielding spirit of its passionate supporters.

Boca Juniors' Libertadores campaign began in the group stage—a crucible where the mettle of champions is first tested. Drawn into a group with teams with rich footballing heritage; Uruguay's Peñarol and Defensor Sporting, as well as bitter rivals River Plate who were out to seek revenge from the previous year's final game in the Nacional Championship. Boca approached these opening games with cautious optimism and a well-drilled tactical plan. The early matches were not simply contests of skill; they were strategic chess matches in which every pass, every movement off the ball, and every defensive line shift had to be executed flawlessly. In the early days of the tournament, the players recalled the atmosphere at La Bombonera, where the roar of the crowd provided both solace and a spur to greatness.

There was an undeniable belief that, armed with their distinctive blend of aggression and artistry, they could outwit and outplay their rivals. And they did; a 1-0 victory over River was precisely the start they needed. And a Superclásico victory is always sweet, regardless of what competition it's played in. In the next game, Boca played out a 0-0 draw against Defensor Sporting before turning over Peñarol in a 1-0 away win. The return leg against Defensor witnessed Boca gain a crucial 2-1 victory. Then a fortnight later, Boca would earn a much deserved 2-0 win against Peñarol. Seven days later, the Monumental was to host yet another Superclásico which finished out 0-0. But it was already enough. Boca topped the group with 10 points, River were runners-up on just 6 points.

The next phase was a semi final. But instead of being a one or two-legged knockout affair, the nature of the tournament meant that it would be contested over two groups of three, with the top finisher of each group playing each other over a two-legged final. Boca were in Group A with Deportivo Cali from Colombia, as well as Paraguay's Libertad.

Boca disposed of Libertad with 1-0 victories both home and away, before drawing with Deportivo Cali 1-1, also both home and away. But it was enough, as Boca finished on 6 points, whereas Deportivo Cali and Libertad both finished on 3. Boca were in the final and there was vast jubilation around the streets of La Boca. Destiny awaits. They would however face reigning champions Cruzeiro from Brazil.

For Boca, reaching the finals of the Copa Libertadores was the culmination of months of relentless preparation, tactical refinement, and emotional sacrifice. The final was to be the ultimate test—a stage where every previous lesson, every moment of joy and despair in previous editions, would converge into a singular contest for eternal glory. The weight of history was palpable as the team prepared for the decisive battle, and the atmosphere within La Bombonera was to be a fortress, electric with anticipation. Every supporter, every former player, and every soul connected to the legacy of Boca felt that the final was not merely a game; it was an event that transcended football itself, a contest that would define the character of the club for generations to come.

In the days leading up to the final, the Boca camp was abuzz with meticulous preparations. Tactical meetings stretched long into the night as the coaching staff, armed with insights gleaned from hours of video analysis and in-depth study of their opponents, crafted a strategy that would maximize the strengths of their own side while exploiting any potential weaknesses in the adversary's game plan. The emphasis was on maintaining possession, dictating the pace of the game, and ensuring that every transition was executed with precision.

The finals were to be played over two legs; home and away. The team that accumulated the most points —two for a win, one for a draw, zero for a loss— after the two legs would be crowned champions. If the two teams were tied on points after the second leg, a playoff in a neutral venue would become the next tie-breaker.

The first game took place on 6th September in La Bombonera. Boca set the tone with a masterful display. Their approach was a synthesis of disciplined defensive organization and an audacious, creative attack that exploited every weakness in the opposition. The players moved with a purposeful rhythm, each pass and counter-attack engineered through hours of meticulous preparation. In the 4th minute, Boca scored the only goal of the game thanks to Carlos Veglio, who slotted home from six yards past a goalmouth engulfed with ticker tape. The stadium roared with the unified voice of a faithful fan base whose chants and songs transformed the venue into a boisterous cauldron. This was a side determined to leave nothing to chance on the continental stage.

The return leg was played five days later at Mineirão, Cruzeiro's 80,000 cauldron of noise, close to the city's artificial Lake Pampulha. The game itself kicked off and was quickly a nervy and tense affair—every move scrutinized by an audience that spanned not only the stadium but the hearts of millions back in Buenos Aires. But it was those same hearts that would be broken 14 minutes from time, when Brazilian international Nelinho struck home from an admittedly excellent 25 yard free-kick. The game finished 1-0, and 1-1 on aggregate. There would be no trophy lifted tonight. The need for a neutral ground was required, and CONMEBOL selected a country wedged in between Argentina and Brazil to host the tie-breaker; the game would be played three days later in the Estadio Centenario in Montevideo, Uruguay.

The stadium has significance for football historians—it was the venue where the very first World Cup final was held in 1930, when Uruguay beat Argentina 4-2. Fast forward forty seven years to September 14th, 1977, a team from Argentina were looking for major silverware to bring back to Buenos Aires. Nothing was going to stop them today. The Libertadores had, at this point, become an enormous obsession for club president Alberto Armando. Runners-up in 1963 against Santos was as close as it got for el Xeneize, and the president could feel it. He needed this trophy. But not just him, the Boca fans needed this trophy too.

From the moment the players took the field, the atmosphere was electric with anticipation and tension. Fans from both sides had traveled to Montevideo, though Boca's supporters, known for their passionate support, filled the stands with a sea of blue and gold. Thousands of bosteros had travelled on ferries and boats across the mouth of the Río de la Plata, from Buenos Aires to the Uruguayan capital to witness the event. They were faced with thousands of Uruguayans in the stadium that night who were loudly cheering for Cruzeiro, who brought a very minimal travelling support. For the players, each step on that pitch was laden with the weight of expectation—not only were they representing their club, but they were also embodying the hopes of the astronomically high numbers of Boca fans back home in Argentina.

The match itself unfolded as a tactical duel on a slightly foggy Montevideo night. Both Boca and Cruzeiro approached the game with a blend of cautious discipline and an eagerness to seize the initiative. Boca, with its trademark combination of aggressive pressing and precise, calculated attacks, sought to impose its style from the first whistle. Their midfielders worked tirelessly to control the tempo, weaving intricate passing sequences to create openings against a well-organized Cruzeiro defence. On the other side, the Brazilians, renowned for their technical proficiency and physical fortitude, deployed a strategy aimed at neutralizing Boca's flair by maintaining a compact defensive shape and launching rapid counter-attacks when opportunities arose. It was a stalemate; 0-0 at full time. Extra time was needed, but those 30 minutes could not break either team. The last step; penalties. By the time the players were preparing themselves for the shootout, the Spanish-born Venezuela-based referee Vicente Llobregat did not allow Boca's coaching staff to enter the pitch to talk with the men chosen to kick the penalties. Therefore manager Juan Carlos Lorenzo took pen and paper to write the names of players designed to kick. He gave the piece of paper to a ballboy and instructed the young Uruguayan to hand the paper to Ruben Suñé. The captain assembled the squad on the pitch and read out what the manager had written. The names scribbled down were Pernía, Tesare, Zanabria, Felman and Mouzo. On the bottom, in much larger letters he wrote the word "abajo" (down) to indicate where exactly the players were to aim when they stepped up. All five Boca players scored. Cruzeiro scored their first four goals, but when left back Vanderlei Lázaro stepped up, he elected to put the ball to Hugo Gatti's left, the eccentric Boca goalkeeper reached in the same direction, saving the shot. Boca won the penalty shootout 5-4 and won South America's most prestigious trophy for the first time.

Club president Alberto Armando got what he was after; the Copa Libertadores. The pain of 1963 had now very quickly faded. Jubilation took over. And that jubilation simultaneously spilled into the streets of La Boca from Boca fans who could not travel. In Plaza Solís, where the club was founded some seventy two years prior, there was a blue and yellow Boca Juniors flag planted firmly in the sacred ground as young *bosteros* from the neighbourhood chanted songs long into the night in celebration. This was the one they had been waiting for. Songs were sung, bottles of beer were drunk, cigarettes were smoked, meat was eaten. Pure bliss in La Boca.

CHAPTER SEVEN

The victory itself demonstrated that in the face of relentless pressure and formidable opposition, Boca could rise above the challenge with discipline and determination. The match encapsulated the essence of Boca's football—where strategy, passion, and courage intermingle to create moments of transcendent beauty. The final remains etched in the memories of the Boca faithful, a beacon of hope and inspiration that continues to define the legacy of the Xeneize.

Boca had a taste of continental triumph. But now they were in with a chance of intercontinental triumph. Since 1960, the Intercontinental Cup was an international football competition, endorsed by both UEFA and CONMEBOL, contesting the winners of the European Cup and the Copa Libertadores over a two-legged affair. Liverpool famously won the 1977 edition of the European Cup, with a 3-1 victory over Borussia Mönchengladbach which meant they would face the Libertadores winner, Boca. The English side, due to a variety of reasons, elected not to participate in the Intercontinental Cup, so the German runners-up, Mönchengladbach, stepped in their place.

For Boca, the change of opponent came with mixed emotions. On one hand, facing a team that had come agonizingly close to European glory meant that the challenge was no less formidable; on the other, it presented an unexpected opportunity to exploit the inherent passion and tactical discipline that had driven them to international success. In retrospect, this twist of fate set the stage for one of the most iconic encounters in the history of the Intercontinental Cup.

Borussia Mönchengladbach, despite not being the European champions, had carved out a reputation as one of Europe's most competitive sides at that time. Their journey through European competitions had been marked by moments of brilliance and resilience, and they entered the final with their own set of ambitions. For both clubs, this tie was more than just two matches—it was an ideological and cultural contest that would determine which style of football would reign supreme.

In the days leading up to the first leg, manager Juan Carlos Lorenzo had sent an associate with a knowledge of the German language to Mönchengladbach's training camp posing as a local journalist therefore given access to watch the German side's training. The deception was nicely executed, as Lorenzo was then provided with a detailed report of their players, their style and technical traits on the pitch.

On a crisp evening, on March 21st,1978, the stage was set for the first leg of the Intercontinental Cup at La Bombonera. As fans poured into the stadium, the air was charged with anticipation and raw emotion. Thousands upon thousands of fans descended on the narrow streets of La Boca in a sea of blue and yellow. The iconic structure, with its steep stands and close proximity to the pitch, ensured that every sound—the boisterous chants, the clapping, and the pulsating rhythm of the drums—felt like an extension of the team itself. For Boca, La Bombonera was hallowed ground, a fortress where legends had been born, and tonight it was destined to witness yet another historic moment.

The game started well, with Boca taking an early advantage courtesy of Ernesto Mastrángelo putting the home side 1-0 up after 16 minutes. Mönchengladbach pulled two back before the half hour mark, with goals from Wilfried Hannes and Rainer Bonhof. Then six minutes into the second half, midfielder Jorge Ribzoli levelled the game at 2-2 in which the game eventually finished.

Between the end of March and the start of May, AFA selected La Bombonera for four friendlies in the lead up to the upcoming World Cup on home soil. Argentina faced Bulgaria, Romania, a League of Ireland XI and Uruguay, winning all four. Unable to secure the Republic of Ireland for the third friendly, AFA managed to arrange a friendly with a League of Ireland XI—a squad from Ireland's domestic league, which at the time wasn't fully professional. Many key Republic of Ireland players were committed to their English and Scottish clubs and were unavailable for an overseas friendly in Argentina. A League of Ireland XI was easier to assemble and, for Argentina, playing a League of Ireland XI allowed them to fine-tune their tactics without excessive risk of injury for the upcoming tournament.

For Boca, they travelled to Germany for the Intercontinental Cup second leg some months later, and the fixture was played on 1 August 1978, in the Wildparkstadion in Karlsruhe, a small city close to Stuttgart and some 350 kilometres from the city of Mönchengladbach. For the handful of visiting Argentines, this leg represented a chance to overturn the balance of the tie and deliver a statement to the European football community. Conversely, Borussia Mönchengladbach, buoyed by the confidence of their home supporters and the belief that they possessed superior technical skills, expected to turn the aggregate in their favor.

The stadium in Germany was a far cry from the boisterous cauldron of La Bombonera. Here, the atmosphere was more subdued, yet the stakes were no less significant. The pitch was immaculate, and the German crowd—while less vociferous than their Argentine counterparts—provided an environment that was both supportive of the home team and indicative of the high standards of European football. Coach Juan Carlos Lorenzo surprised everyone when he decided to replace the experienced 33-year-old Francisco Sa with the younger and faster José Luis Tesare. He also put three attacking players (resulting in a 4–3–3 formation), something relatively infrequent by those times.

The decision was a perfect one, and Boca found themselves 3-0 up before half time, with goals from Darío Felman, Ernesto Mastrángelo and Carlos Horacio Salinas. The final whistle was met with ecstatic celebrations from the Boca players and their traveling supporters, who knew that they had not only overturned the aggregate but had also delivered a masterclass in international football. Another trophy. Jubilant celebrations simultaneously ensued in the noble city of Karlsruhe as well as in the enormous metropolis Buenos Aires - particularly in the *barrío*.

Boca Juniors' success in the Intercontinental Cup had far-reaching consequences. It set a benchmark for international club competitions, demonstrating that teams from South America could not only compete with but also dominate the best European sides. The victory had a ripple effect across the footballing world, influencing tactical trends and inspiring clubs on both continents to elevate their game.

Many Argentinians were enjoying the country's recent footballing conquests. Boca fans especially. Their country not only held, but also won the recent 1978 FIFA World Cup. It was a tournament that captured the nation's imagination amid a turbulent political backdrop. Under the guidance of coach César Luis Menotti, the Argentina national team—bolstered by talents such as Mario Kempes, Daniel Passarella, and Osvaldo Ardiles—embodied a blend of creative attacking football and disciplined teamwork. There were no Boca players in the squad that won the tournament, though Alberto Tarantini did feature. The left-back had recently played the previous number of years in La Bombonera, but due to a contractual dispute with the club, Tarantini found himself clubless by the time of the tournament's opening match.

The military dictatorship in Argentina of the late 1970s used football successes as a tool for propaganda, but for the people, these victories transcended politics. They were authentic expressions of tenacity, skill, and passion. The national team's World Cup win provided a cathartic release for a society in need of pride, while Boca Juniors' international conquest offered a glimpse of the beauty and power of Argentine club football. Together, they painted a picture of a country that could rise above its difficulties through the universal language of football.

As the holders of the Copa Libertadores title, Boca Juniors benefited from a special privilege: they advanced directly into the semifinals. This allowed the club to bypass the grueling group stage of the earlier rounds and conserve energy for the more decisive phases of the competition. Yet, this early exemption did not lessen the pressure. On the contrary, it heightened expectations, as every subsequent match became a proving ground for the Xeneizes' claim to sustained international dominance.

Boca was drawn into a semifinals group that would test their tactical adaptability and team unity. In Group A, the club was pitted against local rivals River Plate and Brazilian side Atlético Mineiro—a challenging mix that required not only technical skill but also psychological fortitude. A Superclásico, regardless of competition, isn't exactly for the faint hearted. For the players, this stage was as much about reaffirming their international pedigree as it was about sending a message to the footballing world: Boca was here to stay at the summit of South American club football.

As a result of their triumph in the previous year in the Copa Libertadores, Boca was poised to defend its title and establish a legacy of continental supremacy. The club entered the competition with a target on their backs. Their campaign commenced in the semifinal group stage, a testament to their esteemed status. Drawn into Group A alongside fierce rivals River Plate and Brazil's Atlético Mineiro, Boca faced a challenging path to the finals.

The opening match in 1978, saw Boca host River at La Bombonera. This Superclásico encounter was a tactical stalemate, with both teams displaying defensive backbone, culminating in a 0-0 draw. This result underscored the intense rivalry and the high stakes associated with the fixture. Undeterred, Boca traveled to Belo Horizonte to face Atlético Mineiro on September 24. Demonstrating tactical discipline and clinical finishing, Boca secured a 2-1 victory, signaling their intent to dominate the group. The return fixture against Atlético Mineiro on October 5 further showcased Boca's superiority, as they triumphed 3-1 in front of their home supporters.

The decisive group match occurred on October 17, with Boca visiting River Plate in the Monumental. In a high-stakes encounter, Boca's strategic prowess shone through, culminating in a 2-0 victory with goals from Ernesto Mastrángelo and Carlos Salinas. This win not only secured their position atop Group A but also reinforced their dominance over their arch-rivals. Concurrently, Group B witnessed Deportivo Cali of Colombia topping their group, setting the stage for a compelling final against the Xeneize.

The two-legged final commenced on November 23, 1978, at Estadio Pascual Guerrero in Cali, in the heart of the city, in front of 50,000 spectators. The match was a tense affair, with both sides exhibiting cautious play, resulting in a 0-0 draw. This outcome left the contest finely poised, with everything to play for in the return leg.

Five days later, on November 28, La Bombonera buzzed with anticipation. The expectations on the streets of La Boca were tangible as blue and yellow flags hung from the windows of apartments and businesses on the nearby narrow streets. The home advantage, combined with the fervent support of the Boca faithful, created an electrifying atmosphere. When 80,000 people crammed into the stadium, Boca rose to the occasion in spectacular fashion. A goal after 15 minutes from Hugo Perotti set the mark that Boca were going to win, and win well. But it wasn't until the second half, in the 60th minute, that Mastrángelo doubled the lead. Then just 11 minutes later Carlos Salinas made it a third for the home side. It was surely in the bag now. But put the final nail in the coffin, with just 9 minutes to go, Hugo Perotti scored Boca's fourth and Cali were dejected. The game finished in an emphatic win.

Copa Libertadores triumph was more than just a title win; it was a statement of intent and a consolidation of their status as a continental powerhouse. This victory laid the groundwork for future successes and instilled a winning mentality that would permeate the club for decades. Moreover, this period marked the beginning of Boca's illustrious legacy in international competitions, fostering a culture of excellence and resilience. The 1978 victory remains a touchstone for Boca, symbolizing the zenith of their footballing virtue and serving as an enduring inspiration for future generations. Boca etched its name in history once more.

There was a name being mentioned consistently during this time in the domestic league, playing for Argentinos Juniors. His name was mentioned in the stands of other stadiums; "you gotta see this kid," people would say. This young man was dominating the nation's sporting headlines by playing the game with such elegance, beauty and determination, scoring goals in almost as many games. He had been capped by the national team, but had been left out of Argentina's squad in the recent World Cup on home soil. There were a lot of eyes on the young guy from Villa Fiorito, then a small yet very poor neighbourhood in Buenos Aires. He was one of the most promising young players, not only in the country, but in the world. His name was Diego Armando Maradona.

CHAPTER EIGHT

On October 31st, 1980, in the newspaper *El Litoral*, Boca's famed goalkeeper Hugo Gatti had quipped "Do you know what worries me? His physique. I have the feeling that in a few more years, he won't be able to contain his tendency to be chubby." This statement enraged young Diego, who had been celebrating his 20th birthday just the day before.

On November 9th, Argentinos Juniors were due to face Boca in La Bombonera. For a fiery competitor like Maradona, this was the ultimate insult. He had already made a name for himself as the best young talent in Argentina, but this gave him an extra edge—an extra reason to prove himself. The match wasn't just about winning for Argentinos Juniors; it was about settling a personal score. Argentinos coach Miguel Ángel Lopez, later told the newspaper *Marca* that this young rising star, Maradona, had looked him in the eye in the dressing room just moments before the two teams were due to take to the pitch, and said "I am going to score four goals against Gatti today."

Boca were favourites going into the match, especially given their home advantage and Gatti's vast experience between the posts. Maradona and Argentinos Juniors, however, had other plans. From the opening whistle, the young Diego was on fire—dribbling past Boca defenders with ease, creating chances, and exuding the kind of confidence that only he possessed. It quickly became clear that he was playing on a different level.

In a thrilling 5-3 victory for Argentinos Juniors, Diego Maradona kept his promise. He managed to put two free-kicks, one penalty kick and a one-on-one chip past *El Loco* Gatti. The goalkeeper later said "I hope that Diego understood me. At no time did I call him *gordito* (little fat guy). I just said he needed to take care of his physique. He's the best player in the country."

THE MOST CURIOUS THING about this is that the Xeneize's fans cheered Maradona. This was unprecedented. Maradona's performance that day, accelerated Boca's desire to sign this young kid. The board wanted him, the players wanted him, and the fans most certainly wanted him. Cross-town rivals River Plate wanted Diego, offering to make him the club's best paid player. But when it comes to negotiations, some things aren't for the money. Maradona harbored a deep-seated desire to don the iconic blue and gold jersey of Boca Juniors, a club he and his family passionately supported. On February 20, 1981, Diego Armando Maradona joined Boca Juniors.

Maradona's debut occurred swiftly two days later when he made his official debut for Boca against Talleres de Córdoba. Despite nursing a minor muscle strain from his final training sessions with Argentinos Juniors, Maradona's determination was unwavering. In front of a fervent crowd at La Bombonera, he netted two goals, propelling Boca to a commanding 4-1 victory. This performance not only endeared him to the Boca faithful but also signaled the dawn of a new era for the club. The season was not without its hurdles. Shortly after his debut, on March 8, Maradona sustained a minor injury, sidelining him until March 29, when Boca drew 2-2 with Newell's at La Bombonera.

One of the most iconic moments of the season occurred on April 10, a Friday, during the Superclásico against arch-rivals River. It was unusual for a game to be played on a Friday in those days, as opposed to a Sunday. The reason being the 1981 Argentine Grand Prix was to take place on the Sunday, with thousands of people due to attend the race in the Autodromo Municipal Ciudad de Buenos Aires, authorities felt best moving the Superclásico to a few days prior to prevent any crowd control problems. In a rain-soaked La Bombonera however, Boca delivered a masterclass, defeating River 3-0. Maradona's goal in this match is etched in football folklore: maneuvering past the legendary goalkeeper Ubaldo Fillol and outsmarting defender Alberto Tarantini with deft feints before calmly slotting the ball into the net. This goal not only exemplified

Maradona's technical flair but also solidified his status as a talismanic figure for Boca.

The partnership between Maradona and Miguel Ángel Brindisi became the cornerstone of Boca's attacking strategy. Though he had not been capped by the national team for some years, Brindisi was an experienced attacking player who the club recently acquired from Huracán. He had also played for Las Palmas in Spain. Together, the pair accounted for 33 of the 60 goals scored by the team during the Metropolitano tournament. Their on-field chemistry was evident, with Maradona's vision and world-class dribbling seamlessly complementing Brindisi's experience and playmaking abilities.

A crucial game occurred on the third last game of the season. Boca were due to face Ferro Carril Oeste on August 2. Both teams were leading the table and in this tightly contested match, Maradona provided a precise assist to Hugo Perotti, and the crowd reaction after the goal is one of the iconic images of La Bombonera; the avalanche. The crowds in the standing section behind the goals, known locally as the *popular*, just rush forward in an uncontrolled surge, crushing together in sheer celebration. It is an intense and chaotic method of celebration and despite the serious risks, *la avalancha* is something of a much loved experience symbolizing unfiltered bliss.

In the penultimate game on August 9th, Boca travelled just under four hours north-west of Buenos Aires, where they would face Rosario Central. Disaster struck as Boca lost the game 1-0. But they knew the final game of the season was just six days away against Racing Club and all they needed was a single point. The match concluded in a 1-1 draw, a result sufficient to crown Boca Juniors as champions. Maradona's contributions throughout the season were pivotal; he amassed 17 goals, making him one of the league's top scorers. This championship not only ended Boca's title drought but also underscored Maradona's transformative impact on the team. The Xeneize had their king.

Following their domestic success, Boca entered the Nacional Championship with heightened expectations. All eyes were on the young kid with the big, curly, dark hair. Not just locally, but the whole world at this point were very, very curious to see what he could do. Maradona continued to display his extraordinary talent, netting 11 goals in 12 appearances. It was clear that this kid was absolutely elite, and there were some comparisons to Brazilian legend Pelé were bandied about in certain parts of the press. However, the tournament then presented unforeseen challenges. On December 6th, in the quarterfinals against Vélez Sarsfield, a contentious first leg saw multiple players from both teams receive red cards. Maradona, reacting to persistent fouls, was among those sent off and was suspended for the next game, to the disappointment of his fellow players and, moreso, to the fans of the Xeneizes. Despite winning the first leg 2-1, Boca were deprived of their star player in the return leg and, such was his impact, they subsequently struggled. A 3-1 defeat meant the club were sadly eliminated from the tournament.

In the early months of 1982, Buenos Aires was a city teetering on the edge. The military junta, led by General Leopoldo Galtieri, faced mounting economic woes and civil unrest. Amid this turmoil, on April 2, Argentina launched an invasion of the Falkland Islands—known locally as Las Malvinas—seeking to reclaim the territory from British control. This bold move ignited a surge of nationalism across the country, intertwining deeply with the nation's most cherished pastime: football.

La Boca, however, always pulsed with life and colour. Its narrow streets, lined with brightly painted conventillos, echoed with the sounds of tango and the fervent discussions of its residents. The smell of coffee, cigarette smoke and different foods filled the air. As the Malvinas conflict unfolded, the atmosphere within La Bombonera intensified. Matches became communal gatherings where national pride and football allegiance merged. Chants supporting the troops were as common as those for star players, and banners proclaiming "*Las Malvinas son Argentinas*" (The Malvinas are Argentine) draped the stands. The war had permeated the fabric of football, turning each game into a symbolic extension of the battlefield.

Boca had entered 1982 with a strong start in the Nacional championship. Convincing wins against Huracán, CA Mariano Moreno and Central Norte gave the club the start they were looking for. The first Superclásico occurred on 7th March, in the Monumental. Boca destroyed rivals River in an emphatic 5-1 victory, with goals from Oscar Ruggeri with one and Ricardo Gareca and Carlos Cordoba with a brace each. The results in the weeks thereafter became a little inconsistent with an unfortunate run of draws and losses. The news of the conflict in the Islas Malvinas had now dominated global headlines.

The ruling junta had always recognized the unifying power of football. In a nation where the sport was akin to religion, leveraging it for propaganda was a calculated strategy. The recent 1978 World Cup, hosted and won by Argentina, had previously been used to bolster national pride amidst the regime's human rights abuses. Now, in 1982, the Malvinas conflict presented another opportunity to rally the populace. The government promoted football matches as patriotic events, with victories on the pitch portrayed as metaphors for anticipated success in the South Atlantic. For Boca supporters (and indeed supporters of other clubs around the country), the war's impact was deeply personal. Many had family members or friends serving in the conflict, and the uncertainty of their fate cast a shadow over the usual matchday exuberance. The terraces of La Bombonera, alive with songs and celebrations on match days, now also felt anxiety from some supporters due to the conflict.

Financial constraints plagued Boca, making it challenging to retain their gifted young player, Diego Maradona. Spanish giants FC Barcelona, one of the world's elite football clubs, some years previously, had sent former player César Rodríguez to see a 17 year old Maradona in action for Argentinos Juniors. Later, in 1979, former defender and Spanish international Francesc "Rodri" Rodríguez also travelled to Buenos Aires to see the young star in the flesh. Both scouting reports were glowing and in winter 1979 Barcelona reached out and came to an agreement with Argentinos Juniors for Maradona to join Barça at the start of the 1980/81 season. English side Sheffield United had also been previously very close to signing the star before Boca did, but their chairman, John Hassell, thought he wasn't worth the money and settled on River Plate's Alejandro Sabella instead.

The Military Junta, however, intervened in the Barcelona deal with Argentinos and prevented Maradona from leaving the country. While he famously signed for Boca, it wasn't until June 1982 that the agreement was made and Diego got his transatlantic transfer in an astonishing-but-not-surprising world record fee. Barcelona got their star, and Boca got some much-needed revenue. Before he donned the *blaugrana* in Spain, Maradona remarked "I have played in the team of my dreams. In the stadium of my dreams." His profound impact not only rejuvenated Boca but also solidified his legacy as one of football's greatest talents.

Less than twenty four hours after the opening match of the 1982 World Cup in Spain as reigning champions Argentina unexpectedly lost to Belgium in the Camp Nou, dawn broke over Buenos Aires, and an unsettling quiet blanketed the city. It was June 14th, and the usual hustle and bustle appeared somewhat subdued, as if the metropolis itself sensed the gravity of the moment. News had spread that Argentina had surrendered to British forces, bringing the ten-week conflict over the Islas Malvinas to a bitter end. The initial euphoria that had greeted the invasion in April had dissipated, replaced by a profound sense of loss and introspection. The war had claimed the lives of approximately 649 Argentine soldiers, many of them young conscripts. The loss reverberated through communities across the nation, turning personal tragedies into a collective mourning. Families had gone to football grounds each week as a means to escape their anxiety and uncertainty that that conflict caused. But now those same families grappled with grief, and the society at large was forced to confront the human cost of the junta's ambitions.

That summer's World Cup, held in Spain, was disappointing for Argentina. While they managed to get out of the initial group stage, the second group stage (a unique format in 1982) placed Argentina in a brutal group with Italy and Brazil, two of the strongest nations in international football. The first match against Italy was a frustrating one. Italy used a disciplined defensive approach to neutralize Maradona, who was to be the focus of the tournament by many managers, players and pundits. Argentina struggled to create chances and lost 2-1, with goals from Marco Tardelli and Antonio Cabrini. With their World Cup hopes hanging by a thread,

Argentina needed to beat Brazil. The two countries had long been sporting rivals, but Argentina faced the Seleção at their best that night, playing beautiful attacking football with stars like Zico, Falcão, and the brilliant Sócrates. Brazil dismantled Argentina 3-1 in RCD Espanyol's Estadio Sarriá in Barcelona, with Maradona getting sent off in frustration after a reckless foul four minutes from time. It wasn't to be. It was something of a humiliating exit for the defending champions.

Back in Buenos Aires, Boca were back into domestic business with the Metropolitano tournament, which was given the name *Soberanía Argentina en las Islas Malvinas* ("Argentine sovereignty in the Malvinas islands"). The team had an enormous Diego Maradona-shaped hole on the pitch, and the signings needed to replace such a player were limited. While there were some great results under coach Carmelo Faraone, with only a handful of disappointing ones, Boca finished third, having won 17 games, drawn 14, and lost 5.

By the following year, the military junta in Argentina had officially come to its end, to much delight. It was a turning point that reshaped the nation's political, social, and cultural fabric. For football fans, it meant reclaiming their beloved sport as a genuine expression of community and identity, free from the shadows of political exploitation. The grit shown during this period serves as a testament to Argentina's enduring spirit and commitment to democracy. The lifting of oppressive measures allowed fans to express themselves more freely. Stadiums became venues not just for sporting events but also for genuine political expression, with chants and banners reflecting societal sentiments and calls for justice. The democratization of Argentina allowed football to return to its roots as a reflection of the people's passions and concerns, free from the manipulations of authoritarian rule.

CHAPTER NINE

By 1984, the music of legendary Argentinian bands such as Sumo and Soda Stereo provided the soundtrack to the country's new political era. However, for Boca Juniors, the financial strains were tangible. Due to safety issues the stadium itself closed before reopening with a reduced capacity. The upper tier of La Bombonera, propped up by large wooden supports, was empty on occasions for fear it may collapse due to the club's inability to pay for the essential maintenance required. The half full Bombonera may have had an effect, as results didn't come the club's way. There was talk of bankruptcies; something that seemed impossible for this gigantic South American institution. Then there were some whispers of actually selling La Bombonera; unimaginable to almost all Boca fans. With the economic issue in utter turmoil, the future looked very uncertain. Supporters were beginning to truly fear the worst.

One of the most ridiculous yet memorable incidents on the disastrous stage occurred on Sunday July 8th, 1984, where Boca played Atlanta, both playing in similar coloured shirts. Atlanta had already taken to the field in their blue shirts. Just as Boca were about to run up the tunnel towards the pitch, an AFA official stopped the players from entering due to the colour clash. A decision was swiftly made for Boca to wear generic white Adidas t-shirts, like ones they would train in, and club staff wrote the numbers on the back of them in indian ink, which would quickly fade into the material following a mix of sweat and rain. They did switch to the home kit for the second half. Boca lost the encounter 1-2.

This was a dark time for the club. As well as being incredibly close to financial collapse, the results simply weren't coming. The club finished 16th in the Nacional, having been eliminated in the Metropolitano. To make matters worse, when Boca were invited to participate in Barcelona's Joan Gamper Trophy, a prestigious annual friendly competition where a club is invited to participate in an exhibition match at Camp Nou just prior to the Spanish side's La Liga season, where they were destroyed 9-1. The demolition job killed morale as it made significant headlines back in Argentina.

Worse was to happen when Boca's finances started affecting the first team. The club's financial instability resulted in unpaid wages, prompting star players Oscar Ruggeri and Ricardo Gareca to protest by refusing to play. This action caused a rift within the team, dividing players into factions. While Ruggeri and Gareca led the strike, others, including Hugo Gatti, Roberto Mouzo, and Roberto Passucci, continued to play despite the financial issues. The two key players however, Ruggeri and Gareca, with the help of agent Guillermo Coppola (who would shortly become the agent of Diego Maradona), wanted to be either paid in full or let go from Boca's books.

Ruggeri had come up within the youth ranks at Boca, and *bosteros* considered him one of their own. While on the one hand, one can see where he's coming from as football as his job and he's not getting what he is owed, in a country where football is deeply cut into society, almost like a religious experience, issuing a strike and demanding to be made a free agent borders on the unforgivable.

Eventually Ruggeri got what he wanted, and became a free agent. But the player definitely did the unforgivable when he immediately joined bitter rivals River Plate alongside Gareca. This was a knife in the heart to the passionate Boca fans. River acquiring the two players ignited sheer outrage. Sadly, in a severe reaction, some supporters set fire to Ruggeri's family home while his parents were inside, though thankfully they escaped unharmed.

Antonio Alegre was a construction worker-turned-prosperous businessman, who had been affiliated with Boca since his youth. On January 6th, 1985, the 60-year-old had been elected to become the president of the club, alongside prominent banking executive Carlos Heller. The pair inherited the club when it was on its knees. One of the first tasks Alegre undertook in office was rectifying some 183 lawsuits from creditors, which burdened the club significantly, as well as La Bombonera's deteriorating condition, which posed significant safety hazards. Demonstrating personal commitment, Alegre mortgaged his business assets to inject US$250,000 into the club and extended an additional US$800,000 loan. These funds were pivotal in settling legal disputes and initiating the stabilization of the club's finances. The president then prioritized the restoration of La Bombonera, recognizing its symbolic and practical significance. Under his leadership, efforts were made to address these deficiencies, aiming to reopen the stadium and restore it as a fortress for the team.

Alegre sought to bring back Alfredo Di Stéfano as the coach of the team, who had previously been in charge when the team won a memorable league and cup double in 1969. The club then secured the talents of José Luis Brown, who had previously turned out for Colombian side Atlético Nacional, to strengthen the team's defence. Joining him was Julio Olarticochea and Carlos Tapia, who both came from River, as a part of a deal that took Oscar Ruggeri and Ricardo Gareca the other way. Two of the opposing players who played for Atlanta in the infamous white jersey match the previous year, Rúben Gomez and Alfredo Graciani, both joined the club also. Emphasis was also placed on youth development, promoting talents from within to rejuvenate the team's core.

Boca participated in the 1985 Nacional tournament. This championship was notable for being the last edition of the Nacional format before the Argentine league transitioned to a European-style season calendar. The club enjoyed some great football, including a 7-1 demolition against Estudiantes on March 6th. Trouble was to find them, however, some four weeks later, when the club faced Independiente in Avellaneda. The game was suspended 6 minutes from the end when a mass brawl took place. Fifty people were injured and over one hundred people were arrested. Police tossed tear gas at the crowd, who were throwing bottles. The fighting continued outside the ground as shots rang out. One of the bullets hit a 14-year-old boy, named Silvio Scassera, who was brought to the Fiorito Hospital where he died. The teenager had been simply attending his first ever football match. A shameful day in the sport.

There was now a new era for Argentine football. The new 1985-86 season heralded a transformative phase, aligning the domestic league with the European calendar. This shift aimed to synchronize national competitions with international schedules, offering clubs enhanced preparation for continental tournaments and fostering a more cohesive footballing ecosystem. The restructuring also included the implementation of a single, unified championship, replacing the previous Metropolitano and Nacional tournaments. This change was anticipated to elevate the competitiveness and organizational coherence of Argentine football.

The league commenced on July 6, 1985, with a convincing 3-1 victory over Racing de Córdoba at La Bombonera, setting a positive tone for the campaign. However, the season was characterized by inconsistency. Notable matches included a resounding 6-0 away win against Gimnasia on July 28, showcasing the team's offensive capabilities. Conversely, a challenging 0-3 home defeat to Independiente on October 20, 1985, highlighted vulnerabilities that needed addressing. The team's form fluctuated, reflecting the transitional phase they were undergoing. The managerial helm witnessed a transition during this season; Alfredo Di Stéfano commenced the campaign as head coach but departed by early 1986. His assistant, Mario Zanabria, assumed the role, guiding the team through the remainder of the season. Zanabria was a former player, who had two previous stints in Boca's midfield.

Despite these inconsistencies, the club managed to secure a fifth-place finish in the league, with a record of 14 wins, 13 draws, and 9 losses, scoring 57 goals and conceding 47, culminating in a total of 41 points, fifteen points behind champions River Plate. The season was a more dignified image than what the club presented in 1984.

Despite finishing fifth in the league, Boca had the opportunity to qualify for the Copa Libertadores through the Liguilla Pre-Libertadores, a playoff system involving top teams. In the qualifying round, the club faced Alianza, securing victories in both legs with scores of 2-1, resulting in an aggregate of 4-2. In the quarter-finals, they met Olimpo and emerged victorious with a 3-2 scoreline. The semi-finals pitted Boca against San Lorenzo; after winning the first leg 2-1 and drawing the second 0-0, they advanced with a 2-1 aggregate. The final presented a dramatic showdown against Newell's Old Boys. The team lost the first leg at home 0-2 but mounted a remarkable comeback in the second leg, winning 4-1 and securing a 4-3 aggregate victory, thus qualifying for the 1986 Copa Libertadores.

CHAPTER TEN

On April 20, 1986, La Bombonera was renamed in honour of Camilo Cichero, the former president under whose tenure the stadium's construction began, symbolizing a new era for the club. But the '85/'86 season was not without challenges. The mid-season managerial change had tested the squad's adaptability, requiring players to adjust to new tactical approaches and leadership styles. Inconsistencies in league performance highlighted areas needing improvement, particularly in maintaining defensive solidity and converting scoring opportunities. However, the team's spirit was evident in their Liguilla campaign, showcasing their determination to compete at the highest levels and their capacity to overcome adversity.

By the end of the Liguilla, the first few games of that summer's World Cup in Mexico were overlapping. The tournament was played amidst concerns over extreme heat and altitude, particularly in Mexico City and other high-altitude locations. Additionally, a devastating earthquake struck the capital in 1985, leading to fears over infrastructure. However, the tournament proceeded as planned and turned out to be one of the most memorable in football history, particularly for Argentina.

In the Argentina squad were two Boca players; Julio Olarticoechea and the young Carlos Tapia. The *albiceleste* entered the tournament with more questions than answers. Head coach Carlos Bilardo had faced fierce criticism for his defensive tactics, his player selections, and, above all, his insistence on building the team around a player who had turned out for Boca just a few years prior; Diego Maradona. Bilardo had long believed that Maradona was not just a player but a force of nature—a singular talent who needed absolute freedom to express himself. There was a portion of people within Argentina who doubted whether such a strategy could lead them to glory.

Argentina reached the final, played on a very warm Sunday afternoon, on June 29, 1986, against West Germany, a team that had ground its way to the championship match with discipline and organization. Argentina started strong, scoring twice through José Luis Brown and Jorge Valdano. At 2-0, it seemed they had done enough. But Germany fought back, scoring two quick goals to level the match at 2-2. The final minutes were tense. The dream was slipping away. Back in Buenos Aires, people were glued to their television sets. The narrow streets of La Boca were uniquely quiet. Everyone was indoors watching this; hoping, wishing, praying. Then, in the 84th minute, Maradona produced his final masterpiece. With the weight of the world on his shoulders, he delivered a perfect pass to Jorge Burruchaga, the former Independiente player who by now was plying his trade with Nantes in France. The forward ran through on goal and slotted the ball past the German keeper, Harald Schumacher. Argentina led 3-2. The stadium erupted. The final whistle blew. Argentina were world champions. Back in the *barrio*, Boca took enormous pride in the fact that Julio Olarticoechea and Carlos Tapia, even to this day, are the only two players, while playing for the club, to have won a World Cup winners' medal.

The 1986/87 season commenced on July 13, with an away fixture against Newell's Old Boys. Despite a valiant effort, Boca suffered a 3-2 defeat, signaling the need for adjustments. The following match on July 20 saw Boca hosting Estudiantes at La Bombonera, resulting in a goalless draw. These initial results highlighted the team's struggle to find harmony and capitalize on scoring opportunities. Boca didn't get their first win until August 3rd, against Deportivo Italiano.

Just before Christmas, Boca were beaten 3-0 at home to Ferro, and Mario Zanabria resigned his position. The club acted swiftly to appoint César Luis Menotti, a manager renowned for his tactical acumen and previous successes, most recently with Barcelona, but also leading Argentina to World Cup glory in 1978. In his playing career, he also had a stint at Boca in the mid 1960s where he won a league title. Menotti's arrival injected a renewed sense of purpose and optimism into the squad.

Under Menotti's guidance, Boca experienced a much-needed transformation. The team embarked on a seven-match winning streak, beginning with a 2-0 victory over Vélez Sársfield on January 25, 1987. This resurgence was characterized by coordinated play, strategic discipline, and an invigorated attacking force. Jorge Comas emerged as a pivotal figure, consistently finding the back of the net and justifying his acquisition.

Earlier in the season, Boca accumulated 23 points from as many games under Zanabria. Under Menotti, however, they managed to get the same amount of points in just the final fifteen games. The title hopes were dashed when they could only secure 2 points from the final three games, and Rosario Central claimed the title, having won the Primera B the previous season. Boca, however, failed to qualify for the Copa Libertadores, having lost the second leg of the Liguilla final against Independiente. Menotti resigned as manager, to the surprise of many, citing personal reasons. But what was more surprising was the coach then signed on as Atlético Madrid manager just days later.

After Menotti's departure from Boca in mid-1987, the club experienced a series of managerial changes in its quest for stability and success. Roberto Saporiti, an Argentine coach with experience in domestic football, was appointed as Menotti's successor. Saporiti had previously worked as an assistant to Menotti during Argentina's 1978 World Cup triumph, bringing a wealth of tactical knowledge to the club. However, his tenure at Boca was short-lived, lasting just five games, one of which was a 0-6 thrashing at the hands of Racing.

The club then turned to Juan Carlos Lorenzo, who returned to Boca for a second stint as head coach. Lorenzo had previously led the team to significant successes in the late 1970s, including Copa Libertadores titles. His return was met with optimism, but the team faced challenges in replicating past glories. His stint was very brief and he left his position just before Christmas. José Omar Pastoriza took over the managerial role in January 1988. Under his guidance, Boca aimed to regain their competitive edge. Pastoriza focused on rebuilding the squad and implementing a more disciplined approach. However, he could only manage to guide Boca to 12th place in the league, where Newell's Old Boys were crowned champions. The club then looked to José Pastoriza to steer the club to its past glories. He was a famous ex-player who had previously won the Copa Libertadores as manager with Independiente.

The 1988/89 Primera División introduced a novel rule to resolve tied games: matches that ended in a draw proceeded to a penalty shootout. The winner of the shootout received two points, while the loser was awarded one point. This system aimed to encourage attacking play but was met with mixed reactions and was subsequently discontinued in later seasons.

Pastoriza's appointment was met with some optimism, given his track record and deep understanding of the Argentine football landscape. That optimism was deflated quickly as Boca lost their opening game of the season against Deportivo Armenia in La Bombonera. The 0-1 defeat turned out to be Hugo Gatti's last match for the club. He had miscalculated a long pass intended for forward Silvano Maciel, leading to the only goal of the game and a 1-0 defeat for Boca.

At 44 years old, Gatti had been a stalwart presence for Boca since 1976, amassing over 417 league appearances and contributing significantly to the club's successes and numerous silverware. This mistake, however, prompted coach José Pastoriza to replace *El Loco* with the newly acquired Colombian goalkeeper Carlos Navarro Montoya in subsequent matches. Consequently, Gatti never returned to official competitive play, marking the end of his illustrious professional career.

Montoya may have been feeling some pressure knowing that the first game for Boca was the following week, and was against none other than River Plate at the Monumental. The game commenced with both teams displaying cautious play, aware of the high stakes and the passionate atmosphere surrounding the Superclásico. As the match progressed, Boca began to assert dominance, creating several scoring opportunities. Their persistence paid off in the 79th minute when forward Walter Perazzo scored a header, giving Boca a 1-0 lead. Building on this momentum, Boca extended their advantage in the 88th minute with a goal from Alfredo Graciani, securing a 2-0 victory over their arch-rivals. However, moments after his goal, Graciani received a red card.

A notable setback occurred on November 20, 1988, when Boca suffered a 6-1 home defeat to San Martín de Tucumán. Despite this, the club displayed persistence, bouncing back from defeats and maintaining a competitive stance in the league. Their ability to secure crucial victories, both at home and away, kept them in contention for the title. The team concluded the season in second place, amassing a total of 76 points over 38 matches. Their record comprised 20 wins, 7 draws, and 9 losses, with the team scoring 56 goals and conceding 38, resulting in a goal difference of +18. They finished eight points behind the champions, Independiente, who secured 84 points.

Under Pastoriza's guidance, Boca adopted a balanced tactical approach, emphasizing defensive organization coupled with swift counter-attacks. The midfield, orchestrated by Claudio Marangoni, served as the engine room, dictating the tempo and linking defence with attack. The versatility of players like Alejandro Barberón allowed for tactical flexibility, enabling the team to adapt to various in-game scenarios. The season had also highlighted the importance of strategic planning and the impact of experienced leadership.

CHAPTER ELEVEN

The late 1980s were transformative for South American football. Traditionally, the Copa Libertadores spanned the calendar year, but logistical challenges and overlapping domestic schedules prompted a reevaluation. In 1988, CONMEBOL decided to reschedule the tournament to the first half of the calendar year, starting from 1989.

Drawn into Group 4, Boca faced familiar domestic rivals Racing Club and Peruvian sides Sporting Cristal and Universitario. The campaign commenced on February 12, 1989, with a goalless draw against Racing Club at La Bombonera. Subsequent away fixtures in Peru proved challenging, as Boca suffered narrow defeats to both Universitario and Sporting Cristal. These early setbacks highlighted the unpredictable nature of continental competitions.

However, Boca's fortunes shifted in the return leg against Racing Club on March 8th. In a thrilling encounter at the Estadio Presidente Perón, Boca emerged victorious with a 3-2 scoreline, thanks to goals from Jorge Comas and Claudio Tapia. Building on this momentum, they secured a 2-0 win over Universitario at home, with Diego Latorre playing a pivotal role. The group stage culminated in a dramatic 4-3 victory against Sporting Cristal, ensuring Boca's progression to the knockout stages.

Advancing to the Round of 16, Boca were pitted against Paraguay's Club Olimpia. The first leg in Asunción resulted in a 2-0 defeat, placing Boca in a precarious position. The return leg on April 12th, at La Bombonera is etched in history for its dramatic narrative. Facing a two-goal deficit, Boca displayed remarkable tenacity, overturning the aggregate score to lead 5-4. However, Olimpia's grit saw them equalize, pushing the tie to a penalty shootout, where they ultimately prevailed, ending Boca's Libertadores aspirations.

Established in 1988 by CONMEBOL, THE Supercopa Libertadores was designed to bring together all past champions of the Copa Libertadores, offering them an exclusive platform to compete for another prestigious title. The creation of the Supercopa not only celebrated historical achievements but also provided clubs with an opportunity to assert their dominance in South American football once more. Teams from the same nation could not be drawn against one another in the group stage, therefore Racing Club, as the reigning Libertadores champions, entered the quarter-final stage, and Boca entered at the same stage after a draw of lots.

Boca's journey began against Racing, the defending champions of the Supercopa Libertadores. The first leg, held on October 19, 1989, at La Bombonera, was a tightly contested affair that concluded in a 0-0 draw. Both teams displayed tactical discipline, with defences prevailing over attacking endeavors. The return leg on October 26th, at El Cilindro, witnessed a more open contest. Boca showcased tenacity and strategic prowess, securing a 2-1 victory. Goals from Claudio Marangoni and José Luis Cucciuffo propelled Boca into the semi-finals, signaling their intent to capture the title.

The semi-final pitted Boca against Brazil's Grêmio, a club renowned for its robust playing style. The first leg on November

8th, at Estádio Olímpico Monumental in Porto Alegre, ended in a 0-0 stalemate. Both teams exhibited caution, aware of the high stakes. The second leg, held on November 16th, at La Bombonera, saw Boca capitalize on their home advantage. With a commanding performance, they triumphed 2-0, courtesy of goals from José Luis Cucciuffo and Claudio Marangoni. This victory not only secured their place in the finals but also demonstrated Boca's growing confidence and cohesion as a unit.

The final of the tournament was an all-Argentine affair, with Boca facing Independiente. The first leg of the final took place on November 22nd, at La Bombonera. In a match characterized by tactical battles and defensive solidity, both teams settled for a 0-0 draw, leaving everything to play for in the return leg. The second leg, just seven days later, in Avellaneda, mirrored the first, with neither side able to break the deadlock, resulting in another 0-0 draw. With the aggregate score tied, the championship was decided by a penalty shootout. Boca held their nerve, converting all their penalties. When Luis Fabián Artime failed to score Independiente's fourth penalty, Boca had done enough, and won 5-3, thus clinching their first Supercopa Libertadores title.

Boca's success in the tournament was underpinned by a blend of experienced campaigners and emerging talents. Goalkeeper Carlos Navarro Montoya was instrumental throughout the tournament, providing assurance and making crucial saves, particularly during the penalty shootout in the final. Defenders such as Juan Simón and Víctor Hugo Marchesini formed a formidable backline, demonstrating resilience and tactical awareness. Midfield dynamo Claudio Marangoni orchestrated play with finesse, while José Luis Cucciuffo's contributions, especially his goals in critical matches, were invaluable. Manager Carlos Aimar's tactical acumen was evident as he instilled a philosophy centred on defensive solidity and swift counter-attacks, a strategy that paid dividends against difficult opponents. Jubilation and bliss ensued back in La Boca, as blue and yellow ticker tape blew down the narrow streets of the *barrio* as, with the help of beer and wine, songs were sung by *Xeneizes* fans long into the night.

In January 1990, Buenos Aires was a city of cultural dynamism and reinvention, caught between the remnants of a turbulent past and the emergence of a new globalized identity. The fall of communism in Europe signaled the definitive collapse of ideologies that had once inspired Argentina's leftist intellectuals, but the country itself was undergoing its own transformation. Argentine cinema, which had flourished in the 1980s with politically charged films like *La historia oficial.* National rock bands remained a powerful cultural force, with bands like Soda Stereo and Patricio Rey y sus Redonditos de Ricota reflecting both the anxieties and defiant spirit of the times. The grand cafés of Avenida Corrientes, once gathering places for political thinkers and writers, now buzzed with debates mostly over President Carlos Menem's economic policies and the ongoing 1989/1990 football season.

Boca at this time faced a series of fixtures that tested their strength and consistency. The team, under the guidance of manager Carlos Aimar, aimed to improve their standing in the Argentine Primera División. Despite facing challenges, Boca's stamina was evident as they navigated through the fixtures. Their efforts during the first couple of months in 1990 were instrumental in securing a respectable position in the league standings by the season's end.

Amidst their domestic commitments, Boca also focused on the international stage, particularly the 1990 Recopa Sudamericana. This annual competition, organized by CONMEBOL, featured a face-off between the winners of the Copa Libertadores and the Supercopa Sudamericana. The team qualified by virtue of their recent Supercopa Sudamericana victory, setting up a clash with Colombia's Atlético Nacional, the 1989 Copa Libertadores champions. Traditionally, the Recopa Sudamericana was contested over two legs, with each team hosting a match. However, due to serious security concerns in Colombia (Nacional had strong links to Pablo Escobar and the Medellín cartel around this time), it was decided to hold the 1990 edition as a single match at a neutral venue. The Orange Bowl in Miami, United States, was chosen to host the fixture on March 17, 1990.

While Miami has a considerable Latin American population, on match day, the 75,000 capacity Orange Bowl witnessed a gathering of only around 9,000 spectators. The stadium was located close to the Miami river, and was used primarily as an American football arena, although an American Soccer League team called the Miami Sharks did use the stadium at this time to minimal crowds. The passionate supporters and curious onlookers who did turn up were very eager to experience South American soccer's fervor. Outside the stadium, there was the unmistakable smell of grilled meat filling the air from the Argentine expats. Inside, the atmosphere was overwhelming, with fans waving flags, chanting, and creating a vibrant backdrop for the players. An enormous flag of Colombia was unfurled in the enormous arena.

The match commenced with both teams exhibiting cautious optimism. Atlético Nacional, known for their fluid passing and attacking endurance, sought to impose their style early on. Boca, however, remained resolute, with their defensive line effectively neutralizing the Colombian side's advances. Midfield battles were intense, with Boca's players working tirelessly to disrupt Nacional's rhythm. Their efforts ensured that Boca maintained a compact shape, limiting spaces for their opponents to exploit. Despite the Colombian side's possession advantage, clear-cut chances were scarce, a testament to Boca's disciplined approach.

In the second half, the breakthrough arrived in the 72nd minute. A swift counter-attacking move saw Diego Latorre receive the ball on the edge of the penalty area. Demonstrating composure and precision, Latorre unleashed a low-driven shot that eluded Nacional's famously animated goalkeeper, René Higuita, nestling into the bottom corner of the net. Boca held on, and as the final whistle blew, they emerged victorious with a 1-0 scoreline, securing their first Recopa Sudamericana title. The title came back to Argentina. One more piece of silverware for Aimar's squad.

Boca concluded the 1989–90 Argentine Primera División season in third place, amassing 43 points, ten behind champions and cross-town rivals River.

CHAPTER TWELVE

The Liguilla in May 1990 was a knockout tournament, usually featuring multiple rounds, but due to the compressed schedule caused by the impending World Cup in Italy, the format was shortened. Only four teams participated in this edition, making it an intense, high-stakes competition for the coveted Libertadores berth.

The campaign began with a semifinal clash against Deportivo Español. In the first leg on May 27th Boca hosted the Buenos Aires-based club at La Bombonera. The match was a tense and tightly contested affair, with Boca's defensive discipline neutralizing their opponents' attacking efforts. A single goal proved to be the difference, as Boca secured a hard-fought 1-0 victory, giving them a crucial advantage ahead of the second leg. Four days later, on May 31, the teams met again at Estadio José Amalfitani, where Deportivo Español sought to overturn the deficit. Boca, however, demonstrated their tactical maturity by maintaining control of the match and securing a 1-1 draw. The result was enough to see them through to the final with a 2-1 aggregate victory.

In the final, Boca faced Independiente, a club with a rich history in South American football. The first leg took place on June 3rd, at La Bombonera. Boca once again displayed their ability to grind out results in high-pressure situations, securing a 1-0 win that put them in a commanding position. The decisive second leg was played three days later in Avellaneda. Knowing that a solid defensive performance would see them through, Boca executed their game plan with precision, frustrating Independiente's attacking efforts and capitalizing on a crucial moment to secure another 1-0 victory. With a 2-0 aggregate win, Boca were crowned champions of the Liguilla Pre-Libertadores and earned their place in the 1991 Copa Libertadores.

With more than half of the Argentina national team's squad plying their trade outside the country for the 1990 World Cup, only one Boca player made the final twenty-two man squad, 30-year-old defender Juan Simón. The world's eyes were on Diego Maradona–then widely considered as the greatest player in the world and possibly of all-time. Argentina suffered a shock 1-0 defeat to Cameroon in the opening match. They did just about recover and advanced to the group stages where they satisfyingly defeated Brazil, then Yugoslavia and then a tense affair in Naples against hosts Italy. The city adored Maradona due to his enormous success with Napoli, creating a unique atmosphere as Argentine and Italian fans clashed in the Stadio San Paolo. Argentina won on penalties thrusting them into the final with West Germany in a repeat fixture of the previous World Cup final in Mexico, four years prior. However, in the final, luck ran out. Missing key players like Caniggia and suffering from fatigue, they struggled to create chances. A controversial late penalty, converted by Inter Milan's Andreas Brehme, gave West Germany a 1-0 victory, marking Argentina's heartbreaking end to a tumultuous World Cup campaign. Boca's Juan Simón played every game for Argentina in the tournament, but sadly could only show a runners-up medal to his team-mates back in La Boca.

The structure of Argentine football has always undergone changes. Following the 1990 World Cup, Argentine football underwent a significant structural change with the introduction of the Apertura and Clausura tournament system. This transition marked a major departure from the traditional European-style single-season format that had been in place most recently. AFA introduced the new format, dividing the league into two separate tournaments per season: the Torneo Apertura (Opening Tournament) was played from August to December, marking the start of the new league format. Then the Torneo Clausura (Closing Tournament) was played from February to June of the following year, concluding the season. The winners of each would be declared the overall champion.

The Apertura started well, with Boca earning four straight wins in a row. However, football's narrative is seldom linear. On September 23, 1990, Boca faced their arch-rivals, River Plate, in a much-anticipated Superclásico. The match, held at the Monumental, proved to be a watershed moment. Boca suffered a 2-0 defeat, a result that not only halted their winning streak but also seemed to unsettle the squad's confidence. This loss marked the beginning of a turbulent phase in their Apertura campaign.

A week after the Sperclásico, Boca lost at home 1-2 at the hands of Rosario Central. The fans in La Bombonera were whistling and jeering manager Carlos Aimar's for his squad selection and decision making at the full time whistle. When Boca visited Newell's Old Boys in Rosario on December 7th, they were outplayed and lost the encounter 1-0. Aimar, despite winning some silverware in recent times, felt he came to the end and resigned his position as manager of Boca. But a week later a tragic incident would occur that would stain the sport in Argentina.

During a match between Boca and San Lorenzo at La Bombonera, a tragic incident unfolded, resulting in the death of Boca supporter Saturnino Cabrera. The event highlighted the severe issue of violence among Argentine football fans during that period. The rivalry between Boca Juniors' "*La 12*" and San Lorenzo's "*La Gloriosa Butteler*" was well-known, with tensions often escalating during matches. On that fateful day, confrontations between the two groups intensified. According to reports, members of the two factions exchanged projectiles from the third tier of La Bombonera. During half time, a six-inch diameter, five-metre-long iron pipe that was ripped from the one of the stadium's toilets where the away fans were situated was thrown from the upper stands, striking Saturnino Cabrera, a 37-year-old Boca member, who was seated in the lower tier.

Tragically, Cabrera, who was a father of three, succumbed to his injuries. The teams did not come out for the second half because of the incident, and later AFA ruled that officially both teams lost the match. Investigations led to the identification and conviction of a young San Lorenzo-supporting individual, who was involved in a prior altercation, and was recognized by his distinctive sweater he wore. Fan violence between clubs' ultra groups, or *barras bravas*, would be synonymous with football in the country over the coming decades.

BOCA FINISHED IN 8TH position in the Apertura. Osvaldo Potente had been installed as caretaker for the final handful of games, but ahead of the Clausura, the club had acquired the managerial services of Uruguayan Óscar Tabárez. *El Maestro* had recently managed the Uruguay national team at the 1990 World Cup. He had also won the 1987 Copa Libertadores with Peñarol. Tabárez would go into the Clausura without the services of Claudio Marangoni who retired to focus on his Escuela Modelo de Fútbol y Deportes, a sports academy dedicated to training and mentoring aspiring young footballers.

Tabárez set out to instil a philosophy centred on tactical discipline, defensive solidity, and swift attacking transitions. His emphasis on a harmonious unit allowed individual talents to flourish within a structured framework. The squad, a blend of seasoned professionals and burgeoning stars, embraced this ideology, setting the stage for an unforgettable season. One of his ideas was to place a young forward called Gabriel Batistuta in a more central role in Boca's attack.

Boca's Clausura campaign commenced on February 24th, 1991, with an emphatic 3-1 victory over Argentinos Juniors at Estadio José Amalfitani. This opening win was a harbinger of the dominance that would follow. The team showcased a blend of defensive zeal and attacking flair, characteristics that became hallmarks of their season. The subsequent fixtures saw Boca maintain their momentum. A 2-0 home win against Huracán on March 3rd, was followed by a resounding 4-0 away triumph over Unión de Santa Fe on March 8th. These early performances underscored the squad's balance and the efficacy of Tabárez's tactical approach.

The midfield trio of Blas Armando Giunta, Walter Pico, and Diego Latorre orchestrated play with a blend of tenacity and creativity. But it was Gabriel Batistuta's performances during the Clausura that propelled him into the spotlight. Batistuta, who would later be nicknamed *Batigol* due to his goal scoring habits, netted 11 goals in 19 appearances. His clinical finishing and aerial technique tormenting defences across the league. Eyes were certainly on this young kid.

The Superclásico against River Plate on March 31st, at La Bombonera, was a tightly contested affair, Boca emerged victorious with a 1-0 scoreline, courtesy of a goal from Diego Latorre. This victory not only bolstered their title aspirations but also reinforced their superiority over their arch-rivals. Any win against River is always welcome for *bosteros*. Another standout performance was the 6-1 demolition of Racing Club on June 2nd. This match showcased Boca's attacking potency, with multiple players contributing to the goal tally.

Boca went undefeated in the Clausura. And despite their phenomenal performances to top the group, the league's structure necessitated a championship decider against Newell's, the Apertura winner, managed by Marcelo Bielsa. Boca were without Latorre and Batistuta, who were away on international duty for the Copa America. Boca brought in midfielder Gerardo Reinoso from rivals River specifically for these games. The two-legged final was a tense affair, with both teams exhibiting tactical caution. The first leg, held at Estadio Gigante de Arroyito on July 3, 1991, ended in a 1-0 victory for Newell's. Boca's hopes were buoyed in the return leg at La Bombonera before a boisterous, sold out crowd on July 9, where they secured a 1-0 win, leveling the aggregate score. However, the championship was ultimately decided by a penalty shootout, in which the side from Rosario triumphed 3-1, denying Boca the overall title.

AFA recognized that the absence of star players to international duty during the league finals was something of a mistake. But it was a mistake they wouldn't be interested in making again. The Apertura and Clausura would be seen as individual tournaments, a trophy the winner of each. Óscar Tabárez's astute leadership filled fans and players with a deep sense of optimism for the future. However, Gabriel Batistute's wonderful performances and goal scoring records for both club and country, enabled Serie A side Fiorentina to sign the young starlet, where he would become a club icon for *I Viola*. Boca brought in Paraguayan Roberto Cabañas from French side Lyon to fill the void.

In the Libertadores, Boca was placed in Group 1 alongside River Plate and Bolivian clubs Bolívar and Oriente Petrolero. The campaign commenced on February 27, 1991, with a high-octane match at La Bombonera, where Boca edged out River Plate in a 4-3 victory. However, subsequent away fixtures proved challenging; they suffered a 2-0 defeat to Bolívar in La Paz on March 12 and a 1-0 loss to Oriente Petrolero in Santa Cruz on March 15. Boca rebounded with a significant 2-0 win over River Plate at Estadio Monumental on March 20. The group stage concluded with two goalless draws at home against Bolívar and Oriente Petrolero. Boca finished second in the group, advancing to the knockout stages.

In the round of 16 and the quarter finals, Boca faced Corinthians and Flamengo respectively with a 4-2 aggregate score in each, to the Argentinian's side's favour. In the semifinals, Boca encountered Chilean club Colo-Colo. The first leg on May 16 at La Bombonera ended with a 1-0 victory for Boca. The second leg on May 22 at Estadio Monumental in Santiago was chaotic.

Following Colo-Colo's third goal, putting them 3-1 ahead, chaos erupted. Disguised as photographers and cameramen, Colo-Colo supporters invaded the pitch, leading to a massive brawl involving players, fans, and officials. The melee halted the match for over ten minutes. The situation escalated to the point where Chilean police, including a German Shepherd police dog named Ron intervened and notably bit Boca's goalkeeper, Navarro Montoya, on the right buttock, an incident that became emblematic of the night's turmoil. Colo-Colo won the match 3-1 when play eventually resumed, overturning the aggregate score to 3-2 in their favour, thus eliminating Boca from the tournament.

By 1992, the club finalized the sale of its ambitious Ciudad Deportiva project. By the late 1980s, the unfinished Ciudad Deportiva had become a financial burden for Boca. Recognizing the club's fiscal challenges, the Argentine government enacted legislation in 1989 permitting the sale of the property, thereby altering its designated use. This legislative shift enabled Boca to divest the land, which was no longer viable for its original purpose. Former club president Alberto Armando, who oversaw the project in its infancy later admitted that his biggest mistake was predicting the enormous complex with the 140,000 seater stadium as its crown would be opened at an exact time and date; 11am on Sunday, May 25th, 1975. The sale of the land further helped Boca's finances for years to come.

In the lead-up to the 1992 Clausura, Boca aimed to strengthen their squad to break an 11-year domestic title drought. Alberto Márcico's arrival at the club was met with enthusiasm, and he quickly became a fan favourite, showcasing exceptional playmaking abilities that added a new dimension to Boca's midfield.

The competition began on February 23rd, with Boca facing Vélez away. The match resulted in a narrow 1-0 defeat, serving as an early indicator of the challenges ahead. However, the team demonstrated their true grit by securing consecutive victories in the following fixtures. A notable 2-0 home win against San Lorenzo on March 1, 1992, highlighted the squad's attacking potential, with Márcico playing a pivotal role in orchestrating offensive plays.

The Superclásico against River Plate on May 3rd, ended in a thrilling 2-2 draw. This high-stakes encounter showcased Boca's competitive spirit and ability to rise to significant occasions. However, the subsequent heavy 3-0 defeat to Rosario Central on May 10th, exposed defensive vulnerabilities and underscored the need for tactical reassessment.

Diego Latorre emerged as a standout performer during the Clausura, finishing as the team's top scorer with nine goals. His offensive contributions were instrumental in several key matches, providing a spark in Boca's attacking third. The club ultimately finished in fourth place, just 3 points behind Newell's, led by Bielsa.

By the end of May, Boca did add a prestigious accolade by winning the inaugural Copa Máster de Supercopa. The competition took place in Buenos Aires, with all matches held at the Estadio

José Amalfitani, home of Vélez Sarsfield, between May 27th and 31st. The format consisted of single-elimination matches, beginning with the semifinals. In their semifinal clash, the team faced Olimpia. The match was tightly contested, with Boca securing a narrow 1-0 victory, courtesy of a goal from Roberto Cabañas. This win propelled them to the final. The final, held on May 31st, saw Boca square off against Brazilian side Cruzeiro, managed by the much-travelled Jair Pereira. The Argentine side emerged victorious with a 2-1 scoreline. Diego Soñora opened the scoring for Boca, and although Cruzeiro's Edson equalized, it was Alejandro Giuntini who netted the decisive goal, clinching the title for the Xeneize.

The club brought in Carlos Mac Allister and Sergio Martínez, the latter known as *Manteca*, to strengthen the squad's depth for the upcoming Apertura. The opening game on September 8th was a disappointing 0-0 draw against Deportivo Mandiyú. But Boca eventually found their consistency. Goalkeeper Carlos Navarro Montoya was pivotal, conceding only 11 goals in 19 matches. He notably saved a penalty against rivals River and maintained an impressive record of 824 minutes without conceding a goal, surpassing the great Antonio Roma's record from 1970.

On December 20th, the final Sunday of the season, Boca faced San Martín de Tucumán at La Bombonera in the final match of the Torneo Apertura. Boca, leading the standings, needed at least a draw to secure their first league title in 11 years, while San Martín sought points to improve their position in the relegation table. The match began with both teams displaying cautious play. However, in the 19th minute, San Martín unexpectedly took the lead. Raúl Roldán delivered a precise pass to Ricardo Solbes, who advanced behind Boca's back four and struck a low shot past goalkeeper Carlos Navarro Montoya, silencing La Bombonera. Shortly after the second half commenced, Boca found their equalizer. In the 47th minute, midfielder Claudio Benetti, in his first and only appearance of the campaign, seized upon a loose ball, evaded a defender, and fired a shot into the net, leveling the score at 1-1.

The final whistle confirmed the 1-1 result, crowning Boca Juniors as champions of the Apertura. This title ended a league title drought for the club, sparking celebrations among players and fans alike. The last time Boca held a league title in their famous stadium was when a young Diego Maradona led the Xeneizes to glory in 1981. Jubilation spilled out from the stands of La Bombonera and onto all around the *barrio* and beyond.

CHAPTER
THIRTEEN

With the 1993 Clausura incoming, in an effort to bolster the squad, Boca secured the services of midfielder Alejandro Mancuso and forward Alberto Acosta. These acquisitions aimed to strengthen the team's core and attacking options. Boca's midfielder José Luis Villareal, who was instrumental in their league success, left Buenos Aires for Madrid, when he joined Atlético. His stint in the Spanish capital was short lived, and he returned and joined rivals River. Later, while playing for *los millonarios*, Villareal unashamedly kissed the River badge after scoring against Independiente. An enormous crime for Boca fans, and to this day he has never been forgiven for the act.

As the season progressed, internal conflicts within the squad became apparent. These issues, coupled with poor results, led to the resignation of manager Óscar Tabárez. His departure left a void in leadership, further exacerbating the team's challenges. Following a brief interim period under "*Patota*" Potente, Jorge Habegger assumed managerial duties. Prior to joining Boca, Habegger had achieved notable success, when he led Club Bolívar in Bolivia to three consecutive league titles from 1987 to 1989 and managed Ecuador's Barcelona SC to a national championship in 1991. During his brief stint at La Bombonera, Habegger guided the team to victory in the Copa de Oro Nicolás Leoz in 1993, marking an international achievement for the club. However, his domestic league campaign was less successful, with Boca finishing seventh in the Clausura, recording six wins, nine draws, and four losses.

Enrique Hrabina, the son of Czech immigrants to Argentina, was a former defender and notable figure in Argentine football. Following Habegger's brief tenure as the manager of Boca Juniors, Hrabina was put in charge of the Xeneize on an interim basis. He oversaw a single game, in which Boca drew 1-1 against Rosario Central, before the news of the new permanent manager would be none other than former manager César Luis Menotti.

El Flaco had most recently managed the Mexico national team, and his return to La Boca was met with widespread anticipation and high expectations. Menotti was synonymous with an attacking, aesthetically pleasing style of play that had brought Argentina its World Cup victory in 1978. Famously, he had previously managed Boca in the 1986-87 season, during which he implemented his distinct football ideology but fell short of delivering major trophies.

To bolster the squad, Boca secured the services of several notable players. Raúl Peralta and Julio Saldaña were brought in to strengthen the midfield, while the attack was reinforced with the acquisitions of Rubén Fernando Da Silva and the return of club legend Alfredo Graciani. Additionally, the defence saw the inclusion of Ecuadorian center-back Raúl Noriega and Uruguayan midfielder Marcos Tejera. These signings were aimed at adding depth and versatility to the team. Conversely, the club bid farewell to influential figures such as Roberto Cabañas and Blas Giunta, marking the end of an era and signaling a new direction under Menotti's leadership

Boca began their Apertura campaign on September 12, 1993, with a home fixture against Estudiantes at La Bombonera. Despite the noise being utterly deafening, the match concluded in a goalless draw. The following week, Boca faced Huracán and suffered a 2-0 defeat, raising early concerns about the squad's balance and ability to implement the new playing style. However, the team quickly rebounded, securing a 1-0 victory over San Lorenzo on September 26th.

October 17th was the date for the Superclásico, and the two giants, Boca and River, clashed at the Monumental. In a tightly contested match, the Xeneizes emerged victorious with a 1-0 win, courtesy of a goal from Alberto Acosta. This triumph not only boosted the team's morale but also solidified Menotti's position, as defeating River is often seen as a litmus test for any Boca manager.

As the season progressed, Boca began to exhibit greater coordination and attacking play. A notable performance came on March 13th, 1994, when they dismantled Racing with a resounding 6-0 victory at La Bombonera. *Manteca* Martínez was the standout performer, netting a hat-trick and demonstrating his clinical finishing abilities. This match epitomized Menotti's vision of free-flowing, attacking football and served as a statement to the rest of the league. The team's offensive capabilities were further highlighted in subsequent matches, with Martínez continuing his goal-scoring spree, ultimately finishing as the tournament's top scorer with 12 goals.

The Apertura title race was fiercely contested, with several teams vying for the championship. Boca's resurgence under Menotti positioned them as strong contenders. However, despite their improved performances, inconsistency frustratingly hindered their title aspirations. The team finished the tournament with eight wins, six draws, and five losses, accumulating 30 points. This tally placed them just behind the champions, River, who clinched the title with a narrow margin.

The 1994 Clausura marked a period of both anticipation and turbulence for Boca. Building upon the foundation laid in the previous season, the club sought to enhance their attacking prowess by signing two forwards: John Jairo Tréllez from Colombia and Ivo Basay from Chile. By this stage, Juan Simón wasn't rated by Menotti, and had retired. Boca seemed uninspired. They only managed to score 25 goals in 19 matches. That summer's World Cup which occurred in the middle of the Clausura, witnessed Diego Maradona's final tournament, which was supposed to be his renaissance and lead Argentina to glory once more. Instead, it finished with him being led off the pitch only to fail a dope test. Argentina would subsequently be eliminated in the round of 16 at the hands of Romania in the Rose Bowl, in Pasadena.

Diego Maradona left Boca Juniors for Barcelona for a world transfer fee in 1982. It was in the Catalan capital where he admitted he first tried cocaine. His time at Barça was plagued by injury, firstly with a bout of hepatitis followed by a broken ankle caused by a reckless tackle at the hands of Andoni Goikoetxea, nicknamed *The Butcher of Bilbao*. His final game for Barcelona was in the 1984 Copa del rey final which ended in a mass brawl with punches and flying kicks being thrown around from all angles, with Maradona at the centre of it all. He was sold to Napoli, an unusual choice for a player of his calibre as Italian football had been dominated by teams from the north and centre, such as Juventus and AC Milan and AS Roma. No team from the southern end of the peninsula had ever won a league title. Maradona changed that and led Napoli to win two *scudetti*, a Coppa Italia, a Supercoppa Italiana and UEFA cup titles. It was in Italy where he cemented his place as the world's greatest player, and by considerable distance. Controversy would find him however, following reports, later proved to be true, of an illegitimate son with an Italian woman as well as his friendship with the Camorra crime syndicate. After his departure from Napoli in 1992, following a 15-month ban for cocaine use, Maradona's journey took him to Sevilla in Spain and later to Newell's Old Boys before two short yet unsuccessful stints in management.

In 1995, an opportunity presented itself that Diego would never forgive himself if he missed it; a return to Boca. Negotiations for his return were complex. Maradona initially desired a dual role as player and coach, but the club's administration, led by club president Antonio Alegre, was hesitant. Financial constraints further complicated matters, as the club was not in a position to meet Maradona's substantial salary demands. However, a consortium of businessmen, including media mogul Eduardo Eurnekian, intervened to facilitate his return. Maradona agreed to rejoin solely as a player, setting the stage for one of the most anticipated comebacks in football history.

Maradona had now been training incredibly hard, in anticipation for the expiry of the 15-month ban. The moment finally came, when on Sunday 7th October 1995, Diego Armando Maradona walked out on the pitch of La Bombonera as a Boca player, the first time in thirteen years. His return to competitive play in the Argentine Primera División was met with enormous anticipation. Maradona was now sporting a bleached blonde streak in his hair, and a goatee beard, when he led the Xeneize out to a 1-0 victory over Colón. He was selected for a "random" drug test at the final whistle. The following week, Boca faced Argentinos Juniors at

Vélez Sársfield's ground. Argentinos gave the young Diego his start in professional football, so when the number 10 scored a free kick, twenty minutes from time, he respectfully declined to celebrate.

THE TEAM CONTINUED this momentum with a 2-1 win over Gimnasia de Jujuy on October 18th. However, a goalless draw against San Lorenzo on October 22nd at La Bombonera momentarily halted their winning streak. Undeterred, Boca secured a 1-0 away victory over Belgrano on October 28th and a crucial 1-0 home win against Vélez Sársfield on November 5th. An away win against Gimnasia on November 9th and a 2-0 triumph over Banfield on November 12th further solidified their position at the league's summit.

One of the matches Maradona was most looking forward to was the Superclásico at the Monumental on November 26th. He and his family had long been Boca fans, even before he was a player, so a goal against River during his triumphant return would be the icing on the cake. It wasn't to be as the game played out a 0-0 draw, but Boca still maintained their unbeaten run. At the final whistle, dozens of journalists, photographers and television cameramen surrounded the 35-year-old genius.

Following the Superclásico, Boca experienced a decline in form. On December 3rd, they suffered a shocking 4-6 home defeat to Racing. This match exposed defensive frailties in what was expected to be a routine win. The subsequent fixtures compounded their woes: a 2-1 away loss to Estudiantes on December 9th and a 2-2 home draw against Deportivo Español on December 16th. These results saw the team relinquish their lead, with Vélez Sársfield capitalizing to clinch the championship, having won their final six games.

Mauricio Macri was a qualified engineer, and president of a company called Sevel, which manufactured Peugeots and Fiats in Argentina, when he was elected president of Boca in December 1995, at 36-years-old. His involvement with the club began earlier, notably through financial support and attempts to influence its direction. Macri's election marked a shift towards a more corporate approach in the club's management. The young buisnessman's initial attempts to influence the club's direction included financial support, such as paying the salary of coach César Luis Menotti and facilitating player acquisitions, including forward Walter Perazzo. His campaign for the Boca presidency was characterized by strategic outreach and coalition-building. Initially, he approached former club presidents Antonio Alegre and Carlos Heller, proposing collaboration to rejuvenate the club. However, both declined his overtures. Undeterred, Macri sought support from various factions within the club, eventually securing enough backing to contest the internal elections. During his presidency campaign, he had received support from numerous notable former players, as well as vocal support from Boca's *barra brava*.

Upon assuming the presidency, Macri implemented several reforms aimed at modernizing the club's operations. He would oversee the refurbishment of La Bombonera, enhancing its facilities to improve the matchday experience for fans and players alike. Additionally, under his leadership, Boca constructed the Estadio Luis Conde, commonly known as "*La Bombonerita*," which became the home for the club's basketball and volleyball teams, located very close to their football stadium.

On the pitch, Macri made the strategic decision to appoint Carlos Bilardo as the head coach. Maradona and Bilardo shared a storied history, having achieved World Cup success together in 1986. However, their relationship had deteriorated during their time at Sevilla, leading to tensions. Maradona initially opposed Bilardo's appointment at Boca Juniors, threatening to leave the club if Bilardo assumed the managerial role. However, he eventually decided that would stay for the sake of his fans and his family.

Under Bilardo's management, the team showed moments of promise but struggled with consistency. The Clausura 1996 season saw Boca finishing in fifth place, with notable performances including a 4-1 victory over arch-rivals River. However, the team also suffered significant defeats, such as the infamous shock 0-6 home loss to Gimnasia, with goals from Guillermo Barros Schelotto who emerged as the standout performer, netting a hat-trick, as well as a penalty converted by former Boca favourite *Beto* Márcico.

Boca's star player Maradona's form fluctuated during this period, and his struggles with fitness and off-field issues continued to be a concern. He returned to form with a comfortable 4-1 over former club Argentinos Juniors, but suffered a muscle injury that put the star on the sidelines once again. When he returned on June 9th, against Belgrano, Maradona scored the opening goal, marking his final official goal from open play. He had received the ball near the edge of the penalty area, deftly chipped it over an advancing defender, and from an awkward angle struck a precise left-footed chip over the goalkeeper into the goal, echoing the moments of genius that the player was synonymous with throughout his entire career.

The following week, Boca faced Vélez Sarsfield at the Estadio José Amalfitani. The encounter started positively for Boca when Claudio Caniggia scored with a header in the 15th minute, giving the visitors an early lead. Having come through the youth ranks at bitter rivals River, he was signed by Boca at Maradona's request following spending several seasons in Europe, mostly in Italy's Serie A. Despite Cannigia's early goal, Vélez responded promptly, with Patricio Camps equalizing, also with a header, just five minutes later. By half time, Boca were without Néstor Fabbri and star player Maradona, who were both sent off. The match concluded with Boca's Carlos Mac Allister also receiving a red card in the 89th minute, compounding the team's woes, as they lost the game 1-5. The following month, Boca defeated River 4-1 in La Bombonera, a game in which Maradona missed a penalty. The team then set out to China to play Beijing Guoan and then Sichuan Quanxing; two friendly in as many days, some 2000 kilometres apart from each other.

When the Clausura resumed three weeks later, Boca were defeated by Racing 0-1. In this game Maradona had missed another penalty, his fifth in a row. Four days later, Boca lost in a 1-2 home loss to Estudiantes, with the away side's goals coming from a young Martín Palermo. Manager Bilardo had stated that the unnecessary trip to China had ruined the squad's momentum. Boca finished fifth in the table, with Vélez being crowned as champions.

At this time, Diego Maradona publicly acknowledged his ongoing battle with drug addiction. In an interview with the Argentine magazine *Gente*, he candidly stated, "I was, I am, and I always will be a drug addict," highlighting the persistent nature of his struggle. In August of that year, seeking to overcome his addiction, he had traveled to Switzerland to enroll in a rehabilitation program at the Bellelay Clinic. He expressed a desire to seek help and control over his addictions, emphasizing the importance of this for the sake of his two young daughters. Maradona chose this Swiss facility based on a friend's recommendation, expressing concerns about the effectiveness of treatment options in Argentina. His stay at the clinic lasted just ten days. Striker Claudio Cannigia also at this time took a break from the game, following the tragic death of his mother, who took her own life by jumping from the balcony of her fifth floor apartment in Buenos Aires. Her funeral, shamefully, became a media spectacle.

Without Maradona and Cannigia, Carlos Bilardo significantly changed the squad as they entered the 1996 Apertura. Key players such as Carlos Mac Allister left while almost a dozen were brought in, including a return for Diego Latorre. On November 3rd, Bilardo's Boca lost at home to Independiente, who were being managed by César Luis Menotti. One of the debates in Argentina was which World Cup-winning manager had the better philosophy. After the encounter managed by the two managers, the Colombian goalkeeper said that he sided with Menotti in this argument. He played his last game for the *Xeneizes* in a 1-3 loss to Banfield, and would be replaced with Sandro Guzmán. *El Mono*, the much-loved goalkeeper and the Footballer of the year in Argentina in 1994, left Boca, joining CF Extremadura in Spain's La Liga.

A week after the Independiente loss, a young 18-year-old made his debut against Unión in a 2-0 victory. His name was Juan Román Riquelme. He was the eldest of eleven children, raised in a working-class family in Don Torcuato, a humble neighbourhood in the northern part of Greater Buenos Aires. His family was deeply passionate about football, and Riquelme developed his love for the game playing on the streets and in local youth teams. As a child, he was a fan of Boca, however, his footballing journey began in the youth ranks of Argentinos Juniors. His technical ability and intelligence on the ball stood out from an early age, and he quickly climbed through the youth ranks, earning the reputation of a very promising playmaker. When Boca acquired Riquelme from Argentinos Juniors, he was brought in as part of the club's future, and in his debut his performance hinted at the playmaker he would later become—dictating play, finding spaces, and distributing passes with effortless precision.

Bilardo left the club in December 1996. And former defender Francisco Sá took charge for the final two games of the season. Boca finished the season in a lowly 10th place. Despite the many transfers that the club had been engaged with at the start of the competition, it didn't gel together to get the results the players were capable of. President Mauricio Macri then installed the managerial services of Héctor *"Bambino"* Veira, who had been managing San Lorenzo for the previous four years.

Veira's arrival was accompanied by strategic reinforcements aimed at bolstering the squad's competitiveness. Goalkeeper Roberto Abbondanzieri returned from his loan spell at Rosario Central, bringing stability between the posts. Midfielder Christian Traverso and winger Alfredo Berti were notable additions, expected to inject creativity and flair into the midfield. Forward Pedro

González also joined the ranks, aiming to enhance the team's attacking options.

The Clausura commenced on February 23rd, 1997, with a 2-1 victory over Estudiantes at La Bombonera, signaling a positive outset. The initial optimism was dampened by subsequent matches, including a 0-1 defeat to Colón and a 1-1 draw against Lanús. A significant blow came with a 0-4 loss to San Lorenzo. Frustrations grew after that campaign's Superclásico at the Monumental. Boca initially surged to a 3-0 lead, with Sergio "*Manteca*" Martínez netting two goals. However, River Plate mounted a remarkable comeback and the game finished at 3-3.

Despite the team's inconsistent form, individual brilliance shone through, particularly from Uruguayan forward "*Manteca*" Martínez. He emerged as the top scorer of the Clausura, netting 15 goals in as many appearances. His remarkable consistency provided a silver lining in an otherwise turbulent season. Soon after, he left for Deportivo La Coruña in Spain. Boca ultimately finished the Clausura in 9th place, amassing 25 points from 19 matches, with six wins, seven draws, and six losses. A very significant highlight of that campaign was the return of the club's icon Diego Maradona. His comeback on June 13th, in a fixture against Racing Club at La Bombonera, whose pitch was caked over from white ticker tape, was met with widespread enthusiasm from fans and players alike. Cannigia also returned, following eighteen months without gracing a pitch for the Xeneizes.

Boca further bolstered its lineup for the 1997 Apertura with the acquisition of Martín Palermo from Estudiantes, the Barros Schelotto twins—Guillermo and Gustavo—from Gimnasia, Colombian stalwarts Jorge Bermúdez and goalkeeper Óscar Córdoba, defender Walter Samuel from Newell's Old Boys, and the Peruvian midfielder Nolberto Solano from Sporting Cristal.

The club started the campaign well. After a thrilling 4-2 victory over Argentinos Juniors at La Bombonera on August 24th. Maradona scored from the penalty spot, and unlike on the previous occasion where he scored against his former team, Boca's number 10 was enormously animated in his celebrations. Boca were playing optimistically, picking up seven points from the first nine available.

The Xeneizes enjoyed a 2-1 triumph against arch-rivals River Plate at the Monumental on October 25, 1997. At half-time Maradona was substituted off, with the young Juan Román Riquelme taking his place. This would be the final 45 minutes of professional football that the great Maradona would ever play. Boca's star had tested positive for cocaine from a recent sample he gave after the Argentinos Juniors game. Diego claimed he was innocent, but on his 37th birthday—Thursday the 30th of October, 1997—Diego Armando Maradona announced that he was retiring for good. This decision marked the end of a remarkable career that had seen both extraordinary highs and challenging lows. The little kid from humble beginnings in Villa Fiorito went to the very top, inspiring millions more to do their best to try to follow in those footsteps. For many, he was the very best.

Boca finished the 1997 Apertura with significant optimism, finishing in second place just a single point behind rivals River. Following Maradona's retirement, they lost their next game against Lanús 0-1. But then went the rest of the season undefeated: Boca secured victories against Huracán, Gimnasia, and Gimnasia y Tiro. The final match, just four days before Christmas, was an emphatic 4-0 home victory over Unión.

For the following Clausura, the club bolstered its squad by signing Colombian midfielder Mauricio *"Chicho"* Serna from Atlético Nacional, Rodolfo Cardoso from Hamburg, and defender Sergio Castillo from Deportivo Español. The competition commenced on February 19th, 1998, with Boca facing Argentinos Juniors away. The team showcased a dominant performance, securing a 3-1 victory with goals from Diego Latorre and Martín Palermo. This promising start was, however, followed by an unexpected 0-4 home defeat to Platense on February 22nd, a result that stunned La Bombonera on that particular Sunday. Just three days later, Boca travelled to Rosario, where they clinched a 2-4 win over Newell's. However, inconsistency plagued the squad, as evidenced by a 2-3 home loss to Vélez Sársfield on February 28th and a 1-2 defeat to San Lorenzo a week later.

That season's Superclásico against River Plate on April 11th was played at La Bombonera, the match lived up to its billing. The Xeneize emerged victorious with a 3-2 scoreline, with goals from Palermo, Claudio Caniggia, and Rodolfo Arruabarrena. However, the euphoria from the Superclásico victory was short-lived. The team suffered a series of disappointing results, including a 1-2 loss to Lanús just three days later, as well as a heavy 1-4 defeat to Ferro Carril Oeste towards the end of the month. Boca's finished with a sixth-place finish with 29 points from 19 matches. The conclusion of the Clausura marked the end of Héctor *"Bambino"* Veira's tenure as head coach. Several players also concluded their stints with the club during this period. Notably, Diego Latorre, Néstor Fabbri, Claudio Caniggia, and Nolberto Solano all left La Boca.

CHAPTER FOURTEEN

Club president, Mauricio Macri, identified Carlos Bianchi, a manager with a proven track record, as the ideal candidate to lead Boca's resurgence. Bianchi's illustrious tenure with Vélez Sarsfield, where he secured multiple league titles and a Copa Libertadores, made him a coveted figure in all of South American football. The man, known affectionately as *El Virrey*, was a famous former player, having played for Vélez, as well as several years in France for clubs such as PSG, Reims and Strasbourg, where he was a prolific goalscorer.

Negotiations began in a hotel in Spain, in the spring of 1998. Bianchi signed a contract with the club, set to commence in July 1998, marking the beginning of a new era for the Xeneizes. The announcement was met with widespread optimism from fans and pundits alike, who viewed Bianchi's appointment as a strategic move towards reclaiming domestic and continental success.

El Virrey brought in some notable signings including right-back Hugo Ibarra, forward Antonio Barijho, and midfielder José Pereda. Additionally, the experienced midfielder José Basualdo, who had known Bianchi from their time together at Vélez, returned to the club, further strengthening the team's depth. But it was 20-year-old Juan Román Riquelme, who the manager saw great importance in.

It was almost two years since Riquelme replaced Maradona at half time, in the latter's last ever professional match. Later, many would see this substitution as symbolic and labelled Riquelme as "the new Maradona"–a term that would be thrown about a bit too easily over the years until Lionel Messi, who Maradona named as his "successor", would be widely regarded as the true custodian of the title.

Bianchi and Riquelme had an excellent relationship. And the coach put emphasis on the 20-year old in an attacking trio along-side Guillermo Barros Schelotto and Martín Palermo for the forth-coming Apertura. Defensively, the team was anchored by the for-midable partnership of Jorge Bermúdez and Walter Samuel, with Óscar Córdoba providing reliability in goal. The full-back posi-tions, manned by Hugo Ibarra and Rodolfo Arruabarrena, offered both defensive solidity and offensive support.

The new coach's first match was on August 5th, with a home match against his former club Vélez, where they suffered a narrow 0-1 defeat in the Copa Mercosur, a club competition featuring top teams from Argentina, Brazil, Uruguay, Chile, and Paraguay, which Boca crashed out in the quarter-finals against Palmeiras. The com-petition wasn't a priority for Bianchi, as evidenced by his team se-lections.

The Apertura campaign commenced four days after the Vélez defeat, with Boca securing a 4-2 victory against Ferro. Boca's attack-ing strength was on full display the following month in a 6-2 home victory over Huracán. It was a game full of beautiful football, with goals from Fernando Navas, two from Martín Palermo, Christian Giménez, Guillermo Barros Schelotto, and José Basualdo highlighted their offensive depth.

Continuing the season unbeaten, on matchday twelve, Boca travelled across town to face River, going into the game six points clear at the top. The game finished 0-0, but the home team missed a penalty from Marcelo Gallardo, and Boca's unbeaten run would continue. In a crucial away fixture the following month, Boca emerged victorious with a 3-1 scoreline against San Lorenzo. Goals from Martín Palermo, Diego Cagna, and Guillermo Barros Schelotto demonstrated the team's composure under pressure and reinforced their championship aspirations.

When Boca faced Independiente on November 29th, it finished out as a 0-0 draw. But Gimnasia had lost to Lanús, which ended their title hopes. Boca were now champions and performed a lap of honour around the famous La Bombonera pitch as jubilation in the stands spilled out onto the narrow streets of La Boca, and fireworks were set off in Plaza Solís, the very park where the club was founded on a bench ninety three years earlier. Pure bliss once more, as it had been six years since the domestic league trophy was claimed by the Xeneizes.

Boca's campaign was marked by an impressive unbeaten run. Over 19 matches, the team secured 13 victories and six draws, amassing 45 goals while conceding only 18. This consistency was a testament to Bianchi's tactical acumen and the players' unwavering commitment. Central to the team's success was the phenomenal form of striker Martín Palermo. He netted 20 goals in 19 matches, setting a record for short tournaments by scoring more goals than games played. Palermo's clinical finishing and aerial dominance made him a nightmare for opposing defenders. Supporting him were Guillermo Barros Schelotto, whose agility and crossing ability provided numerous assists, as well as the young Riquelme, who orchestrated the midfield with his vision, flair and passing accuracy.

The objective for Bianchi was now very clear: repeat the success of the previous campaign. Do not rest on our laurels. Become back-to-back champions. Boca entered the 1999 Clausura with heightened expectations. The club's management, led by President Mauricio Macri, ensured stability by retaining key players and reinforcing the squad where necessary. *El Virrey's* tactical setup revolved around a balanced 4-3-1-2 formation. This system allowed for defensive solidity while granting Riquelme the freedom to operate as an *enganche* (playmaker), linking the midfield and attack.

The campaign didn't begin until March 7th, with Boca Juniors hosting Ferro Carril Oeste. Displaying tactical superiority and clinical execution, Boca secured a 3-0 victory, setting a positive tone for the season. Goals from Martín Palermo, Guillermo Barros Schelotto, and Jorge Bermúdez highlighted the team's ferocious forward line. Building on this momentum, Boca registered consecutive victories against Gimnasia (Jujuy) (2-0) and Argentinos Juniors (3-0) in the following weeks. These performances underscored the team's defensive potency, as they managed to keep clean sheets while showcasing versatility in attack.

Continuing an unbeaten run, Boca faced River in the Superclásico on May 9th at La Bombonera. Busloads of fans unfurled blue-and-gold flags and banners as they entered the *barrio*, to the soundtrack of chanting and the unmistakable drums and cymbals, synonymous with Argentinian football. The encounter began with incredibly high intensity, with both teams vying for control. The Xeneizes struck first, with Jorge Bermúdez heading in a corner to give the hosts the lead. However, the dynamics shifted significantly when Bermúdez received a red card just before halftime, leaving Boca with ten men. River capitalized on the numerical advantage, equalizing early in the second half. Bianchi had no choice but to re-organize his team to absorb pressure and exploit counter-attacking opportunities. This strategy paid off when Palermo, from approximately 25 metres out, unleashed a powerful shot that found the back of the net, securing a 2-1 victory for Boca.

Boca extended their unbeaten run to 40 matches, surpassing the previous record held by Racing since the 1960s. Just four days later, the team suffered a heavy 4-0 defeat to Independiente, ending their remarkable streak. Despite this setback, arch-rivals River's loss on the same ensured that Boca clinched the Clausura title. The *bi-campeones* finished seven points ahead of their rivals, scoring 35 goals whilst conceding only 11 in 19 games. Jubilation ensued in La Boca that night, and once more when Boca faced Lanús in their final home game of the season the following week.

Boca went into the following Apertura hungry, and immediately took revenge on Independiente for ending their 40 match un-beaten streak by walloping them 3-0 at home on the opening day of the campaign. The following match on August 18 saw Boca host-ing Racing. Despite dominating possession and creating numer-ous scoring opportunities, Boca was held to a 1-1 draw. This result served as a reminder of the unpredictability of football and the ne-cessity for clinical finishing in front of goal. Undeterred by the ear-ly draw, Boca embarked on a series of impressive performances. On August 22nd, faced Lanús away and secured a resounding 4-1 vic-tory. The team's offensive fluidity was on full display, with Paler-mo continuing his goal-scoring form and the midfield orchestrat-ing play with precision. The momentum continued a week later, as Boca hosted newly promoted Chacarita Juniors. Demonstrating their superiority, Boca clinched a deserved 2-0 win, with two goal from Guillermo Barros Schelotto.

As the season progressed, Boca encountered challenges that tested them. Injuries to key players, including defender Walter Samuel and midfielder Diego Cagna, necessitated tactical adjustments. Bianchi's ability to adapt was evident as he integrated squad players into the starting lineup without compromising the team's performance. A test came on September 19th, when Boca faced Vélez Sarsfield away. Despite a valiant effort, Boca suffered a 3-1 defeat, marking their first loss of the season. This result served as a wake-up call, emphasizing the need for consistency in a highly competitive league. Boca finished the season in third position, just 3 points behind champions River. But with the talent in the squad, including the supremely gifted Juan Román Riquelme and 1998's Argentina Player of the Year, the incredibly prolific Martín Palermo, there was a sense that Bianchi's best work was yet to come. The focus would shift to the Libertadores.

The club's last Copa Libertadores triumphs were in 1977 and 1978, and the new millennium presented an opportune moment to reclaim continental supremacy. Boca were drawn into Group 2 alongside Peñarol (Uruguay), Blooming (Bolivia), and Universidad Católica (Chile). The campaign commenced on February 23rd 2000, with an unexpected setback—a 1-0 defeat to Blooming in Santa Cruz.

Responding to the initial disappointment, Boca secured a 2-1 victory over Universidad Católica at La Bombonera. The team then crossed the enormous mouth of the Río de la Plata, where they faced Peñarol at the historic Estadio Centenario in Montevideo, where they earned a hard-fought 0-0 draw, demonstrating defensive strength. The return fixture against Blooming on saw Boca unleash their attacking potential, with the late Alfredo Moreno scoring five goals in a resounding 6-1 victory. Subsequent wins against Universidad Católica (3-1 away) and Peñarol (3-1 at home) solidified Boca's position atop the group, advancing to the knockout stages with confidence.

In the Round of 16, Boca faced Ecuadorian side El Nacional. The first leg ended in a nervous goalless draw in Quito. The return leg at La Bombonera was a thrilling encounter, with Boca emerging victorious 5-3, thus advancing to the quarterfinals. The quarterfinals presented a monumental challenge—a Superclásico clash with arch-rivals River Plate.

Television sets from around the continent tuned into the first leg on May 17th at the Monumental which saw Boca suffer a 2-1 defeat. However, the away goal scored by a sumptuous free-kick from Riquelme provided a glimmer of hope. The return leg a week at La Bombonera became legendary. Martín Palermo had been out for the previous six months due to injury yet he vowed to be fit and ready for the second leg between the two sides. River's manager Américo Gallego insisted that Boca's prolific striker wouldn't have a chance of being fit, let alone playing, stating that if he did in fact play, then he would select club legend Enzo Francescoli, who by then was almost 40-years-old and had been retired for three years. Palermo wasn't fully fit but he was selected as Boca delivered a masterclass performance, winning 3-0. The third goal, naturally, was scored by the striker. Boca's number 9 picked up the ball from beside the penalty spot from Battaglia cross. He took a touch on the ball which wrong-footed Víctor Zapata, who foolishly didn't close down Palermo whatsoever, giving the striker more than enough time to turn and slot it nicely in the bottom corner. The goal became known as "*el gol de las muletas*", the goal on crutches. The goal had Martín Palermo etching his name into Boca folklore and propelling the team into the semifinals.

In the semifinals, Boca faced Club América from Mexico. The first leg at La Bombonera resulted in a commanding 4-1 victory for Boca, establishing a substantial advantage. Boca travelled to the Mexican capital for the away leg, in the Estadio Azteca, the venue where Argentina won its 1986 World Cup, led by club legend Diego Maradona. In the fixture, Boca lost 3-1, but it was the late Walter Samuel header that secured Boca advancing to the final on aggregate.

The final pitted Boca against the defending champions, Palmeiras, managed by Luis Felipe Scolari. The first leg at La Bombonera ended in a 2-2 draw. The second leg at the Estádio do Morumbi in São Paulo was a tense affair, culminating in a 0-0 draw. The championship was decided by a penalty shootout, where Boca triumphed 4-2, with goalkeeper Óscar Córdoba emerging as the hero by saving two penalties. This victory secured Boca's third Copa Libertadores title, ending a 22-year wait. Jubilation ensued from the *barrío* right all the way through to the Avenida 9 de Julio, in the centre of Buenos Aires.

The Libertadores triumph granted Boca the opportunity to contest the Intercontinental Cup, a prestigious fixture that pitted the champions of Europe against their South American counterparts. Their adversary, Real Madrid, had secured the UEFA Champions League title, boasting a squad replete with world-class talent such as Raúl, Luis Figo, Fernando Hierro, Iker Casillas and Roberto Carlos to name but a few.

Real Madrid entered the match as favourites as they were in the very beginning of their *galácticos* era. The Spanish side was perceived as a formidable force, with expectations tilted heavily in their favour. Conversely, Boca approached the encounter with a blend of confidence and pragmatism. *El Virrey*'s tactical acumen and the team's unity were pivotal in their preparations, focusing on neutralizing Madrid's strengths while exploiting potential vulnerabilities.

Approximately ten thousand *bosteros* travelled from Argentina to Japan, for the match held at the National Stadium, an enormous 57,000-capacity bowl of a stadium, very close to the city's Akasaka Place. The match unfolded in a manner that defied the anticipations of many pundits and, likely, Real Madrid manager Vicente del Bosque himself. Within the first six minutes, Boca commenced with an intensity that caught Real Madrid off guard as striker Martín Palermo netted two goals within the first six minutes.

Real Madrid, stunned by the early onslaught, sought to regain composure and assert their dominance and tore into Boca. Their efforts bore fruit in the 12th minute when Brazilian full-back Roberto Carlos unleashed a powerful left-footed strike, reducing the deficit to 2-1. Despite sustained pressure from the Spanish side, Boca's defence, marshaled by goalkeeper Óscar Córdoba and defenders Jorge Bermúdez and Aníbal Matellán, exhibited remarkable skill. Riquelme orchestrated play with poise, ensuring Boca maintained control and mitigated Madrid's advances. One of his free-kicks steadied the nerves as it forced Madrid goalkeeper Casillas to make a huge save, a reminder that the Argentinian side are capable of causing trouble, despite playing a very defensive game. Boca held on for a famous victory. The celebrations in Tokyo among the travelling Boca fans were felt back in the *barrío*, as the time difference meant that the fans back home were celebrating in the morning time. It's never too early for a tipple when your team has beaten Real Madrid in the Intercontinental Cup.

Following success in Japan, fatigue and a congested fixture schedule posed significant hurdles. A narrow 1-0 home win over San Lorenzo courtesy of a Palermo goal, demonstrated the team's grit. However, subsequent back-to-back defeats against Independiente and Chacarita Juniors threatened to derail their title aspirations. These losses underscored the physical and mental toll of their exhaustive campaign. Despite the setbacks, and just three weeks after the success against Real Madrid, Boca wrapped up their domestic Apertura title, as rivals River only managed to scrape a point from their final two games of the season. A triple crown of a Copa Libertadores, Intercontinental Cup and now the Apertura. It was starting to feel like the golden age for *Los Xeneizes*.

Following the extraordinary success of the previous year, Carlos Bianchi said that 2001 would be a year of transition. Martín Palermo would leave for Spanish side Villareal. Players such as Rodolfo Arruabarrena and Diego Cagna had also previously left for the small town close to Spain's east coast. *El Submarino Amarillo* were enjoying success, and many players were naturally in the market for some of the financial rewards that playing in Europe's Champions League had to offer.

In the Clausura, which ran in tandem with the Copa Libertadores, *el Virrey* rotated the squad heavily, using over thirty players in the domestic competition, thus ensuring the stronger players were fit and ready for the continental competition. The outstanding moment of the Clausura is the 3-0 win in the Superclásico. The second goal was scored by Riquelme, who celebrated by cupping his ears and staring directly at club president Mauricio Macri. While the player insisted it was a celebration for his young daughter, mimicking a character from an Italian TV show of which the child was a fan of, it's widely considered it was indeed for Macri, due to a contract dispute. European clubs were starting to get very interested in the young playmaker, and this was music to their cupped ears.

San Lorenzo captured the Clausura crown, with Boca 17 points behind them. All of Bianchi's eggs were in the Libertadores basket. Boca commenced their continental campaign in Group 8, alongside Deportivo Cali from Colombia, Chilean side Cobreloa, and Bolivia's Oriente Petrolero.

Their journey began at La Bombonera, where they faced Oriente Petrolero. The match concluded with a 2-1 victory for Boca, setting a positive tone for the tournament. Subsequently, Boca traveled to Calama to face Cobreloa, securing a narrow 1-0 win. Continuing their strong form, they defeated Deportivo Cali 2-1 at home. Boca then hosted Cobreloa again, emerging victorious with a 1-0 scoreline. Their dominance was further evident when they defeated Oriente Petrolero 1-0 in Santa Cruz. However, their unbeaten run faced a setback on May 2, with a 3-0 loss to Deportivo Cali away. Despite this defeat, Boca topped their group with 15 points from six matches.

Advancing to the Round of 16, Boca were pitted against another Colombian side in Atlético Junior. The first leg at the Estadio Metropolitano in Barranquilla, was a thrilling encounter. Boca showcased their attacking valor, securing a 3-2 victory, which provided them with a crucial advantage heading into the second leg. The return fixture at La Bombonera was a more subdued affair, ending in a 1-1 draw. This result ensured Boca's progression to the quarterfinals, with an aggregate score of 4-3.

In the quarterfinals, Boca faced Brazilian side Vasco da Gama, a team that had been impeccable in the group stages, winning all their matches. The Xeneize delivered a disciplined performance, earning a 4-0 aggregate win, thrusting them into the semis, which presented a rematch of the previous year's final, with the team facing Palmeiras. With the aggregate score tied at 4-4, the tie proceeded to penalties. Goalkeeper, Óscar Córdoba, emerged as the hero, making crucial saves to secure a 3-2 victory in the shootout.

The final saw Boca face Cruz Azul, marking the first time a Mexican team had reached this stage of the competition. The first leg on June 20 at Estadio Azteca was a closely contested affair. Boca managed to secure a 1-0 win, courtesy of a goal from Marcelo Delgado. The second leg on June 28 at La Bombonera proved to be a stern test. Cruz Azul stunned the home crowd by winning 1-0, with Juan Francisco Palencia scoring. With the aggregate score at 1-1, the championship was decided by penalties. Once again, Óscar Córdoba showcased his penalty-saving nerve, and Boca triumphed 3-1 in the shootout, clinching their fourth Copa Libertadores title.

Boca once again became continental *bicampeon*, echoing their previous back-to-back Libertadores victories in 1977 and 1978. Jubilation across the city of Buenos Aires ensued, and especially back at La Bombonera, as fireworks were being ignited on numerous streets, lighting up the *barrío* night sky presenting a multi-coloured explosion of beauty, the colours similar to the nearby Caminito, the world-famous street which lies in the heart of La Boca. The club's victory was emblematic of their determination and adaptability. The team's ability to secure crucial away victories, particularly in hostile environments, underscored their mental fortitude in an era when Argentinian clubs' best players were financially lured by their more powerful counterparts in Europe.

To bolster their defence, the club acquired Jorge Martínez, Rolando Schiavi, and the Brazilian Jorginho. Despite their potential, these additions struggled to match the impact of their predecessors. In a move driven more by marketing than footballing needs, Japanese forward Naohiro Takahara was signed. His tenure at the club yielded minimal contributions, despite numerous Boca shirts being sold in Japan.

The team faced Talleres de Córdoba at the Estadio Mario Alberto Kempes on matchday 10. Carlos Bianchi handed a debut to an incredibly promising forward by the name of Carlos Tevez. He entered the field wearing jersey number 18, substituting for striker Roberto Colautti in the 61st minute. It was mother's day, so instead of the Quilmes sponsor that was donned on the front of the jersey, each player would have the name of their mother using the beer company's font. Tevez's jersey had the name Fabiana on the front, his estranged biological mother, as opposed to his aunt, Adriana, who raised him on the tough streets of Fuerte Apache, guiding him towards a career in football, as opposed to drugs or crime that had consumed many of its inhabitants.

Throughout the Apertura, Boca's attention seemed divided, with a significant focus on the Intercontinental Cup against Champions League winners Bayern Munich in the same venue in Tokyo where they beat Real Madrid twelve months prior. The German side featured a large haul of fantastic players such as Oliver Kahn, Giovane Élber, Willy Sagnol, Claudio Pizarro, Niko Kovač and Bixente Lizarazu to name but a few.

Boca were under pressure for most of the game as they couldn't seem to get past the German side's disciplined defence but they held on for the full 90 minutes. Many felt, including some of the players on the pitch, that the Danish referee officiating the tie, Kim Milton Nielsen, favoured decisions to the German side's once too often. It wasn't until the 109th minute, Ghanaian defender Samuel Kuffour capitalized on a corner kick to score the only goal of the match. Despite Boca's bravery, Bayern's physicality and experience ultimately prevailed. It wasn't to be.

Upon arriving back in Argentina, Boca immediately returned to the Apertura, losing to Banfield and drawing with Vélez. Coach Bianchi had announced in a press conference the previous September that he would not be renewing his contract with the club, which expired on New Years Eve. He had been constantly angered by the club's regular sales of key players, as well as the players that the board brought in were not his choices. So when Boca faced Independiente at La Bombonera a week before Christmas, it turned out to be *El Virrey's* final match in the dugout for the Xeneize. Boca won 5-3, while the bosteros chanted Bianchi's name throughout. He led Boca to an unprecedented period of success—including three Argentine league titles (1998 Apertura, 1999 Clausura, 2000 Apertura), two Copa Libertadores (2000, 2001), and the 2000 Intercontinental Cup.

CHAPTER FIFTEEN

The success Bianchi had brought led to Boca opening the Museo de la Pasión Boquense, a state-of-the-art museum located inside La Bombonera, celebrating the club's rich history and achievements. This was a landmark moment for the club, as they became one of the first South American clubs to establish a dedicated museum showcasing its legacy, while tourism to La Boca was always increasing.

Because of the severe economic issue in Argentina at this time, Boca struggled with rising operational costs at La Bombonera, reduced sponsorship revenue, and declining match-day income as fans faced economic hardships. In late 2001, as Argentina's economic crisis deepened, people rushed to withdraw their money from banks, fearing a financial collapse. The country was facing a severe recession, rising unemployment, and an unsustainable currency peg between the Argentine peso and the U.S. dollar, which had been in place since the early 1990s.

To prevent a total banking collapse, Economy Minister Domingo Cavallo implemented a policy known as the "Corralito". This measure froze bank accounts and limited cash withdrawals to just 250 pesos per week, effectively trapping people's savings. The move sparked mass outrage, as ordinary citizens could no longer access their money. Businesses suffered, and Boca Juniors, as a football club, suffered like everyone else. The club played their final Apertura game in February of 2002 without Bianchi in the dugout, forced to move into a new era both on and off the pitch.

By mid-2002, there was a big Carlos Bianchi-shaped hole in the dugout of La Bombonera. And club president, Mauricio Macri, wanted to fill this hole with someone who knew the club and, more importantly, knew success. Óscar Tabárez returned to Boca as head coach, marking his second stint with the club. *El Maestro*, who had previously managed Boca in the 1991–92 season, returned at a challenging time, as the club was navigating the aftermath of Argentina's economic crisis, player departures, and the end of its most dominant era under Bianchi.

Boca entered the 2002 Clausura with effective attacking, scoring 35 goals, but defensive inconsistencies and lapses in key moments prevented the team from mounting a serious title challenge. A low point was the Superclásico against River Plate, played at La Bombonera, where Boca suffered a humiliating 3-0 defeat. The league was ultimately won by rivals River, adding to the frustration of fans who had grown accustomed to dominating both domestically and internationally under the previous manager. The new era started like a bad hangover.

That year's Copa Libertadores was a disappointing campaign for Boca, as they failed to defend their title and lost in the quarter final to Paraguayan side Olimpia. The game was the last match for Juan Román Riquelme. Having established himself as one of the greatest playmakers in the club's history, leading them to multiple domestic and international titles—including the 2000 and 2001 Copa Libertadores—his departure was driven by financial necessity rather than sporting reasons. Boca, struggling with economic issues, accepted Barcelona's €11 million offer despite Riquelme's reluctance to leave his boyhood club.

At the Camp Nou, he was signed by then-president Joan Gaspart, having witnessed just how gifted the young player was. Sadly he was not a priority for manager Louis van Gaal, who considered him a "political signing" rather than a tactical fit. The eccentric Dutch manager, preferring a rigid system, played Riquelme out of position on the left wing, limiting his effectiveness. Meanwhile back in Argentina, *bosteros* and teammates mourned his departure, knowing he had been forced out at his peak.

The departure of Riquelme had left Boca at a crossroads. The club, so used to his effortless command of the game, was now forced to adapt. With Óscar Tabárez at the helm and a new generation of players stepping forward—none more promising than a young, brash Carlos Tevez—Boca entered the 2002 Apertura determined to prove they could thrive without their departed star.

For much of the campaign, Boca remained in the hunt, battling for supremacy in an unpredictable and fiercely contested league. But something was missing. Riquelme's absence was felt in the finer details—the moments of calm when games became frantic, the decisive pass that split a defence, the assurance that no matter how tightly marked he was, Boca always had a man in control.

A joyful *Superclásico* occurred in the Monumental. River were only too happy to derail Boca's title hopes, but succumbed to a 2-1 defeat to *Los Xeneizes* shifted momentum towards Boca. While they remained in contention, something had slipped. It was Independiente—guided by Américo Gallego and led by the lethal eye for goal from Andrés Silvera—who emerged as the champions.

Less than twelve months after his exit, Carlos Bianchi was rumoured to make a dramatic return to La Boca. By Christmas 2002, club president Mauricio Macri and *El Virrey* agreed a deal. The most successful manager in Boca Juniors' history, agreed to return to the club on a three year deal, looking to repeat his previous successes. The news was met with incredible optimism among *bosteros*. The previous season hadn't been a complete disaster under Tabárez, but the prospect of Bianchi in the dugout meant the very real possibility of silverware.

Bianchi's first game in return concluded with a 2-0 victory against Nueva Chicago. It was a functional, workmanlike performance—exactly the type of result that defined Bianchi's teams. The squad had changed since his last tenure, but the core principles remained the same. Goalkeeper Roberto Abbondanzieri had now taken over as Boca's number one, while Rolando Schiavi and Nicolás Burdisso marshaled the defence. In midfield, Sebastián Battaglia provided grit and steel, while Guillermo Barros Schelotto and Marcelo "*Chelo*" Delgado brought flair and intelligence in attack. And then there was Carlos Tevez—young, tough, raw, but already brimming with the kind of talent that would soon make him indispensable.

While Boca's domestic campaign progressed steadily, the Copa Libertadores loomed. The tournament, which had defined Bianchi's first stint at Boca, began in March, with the club drawn into Group 7 alongside Independiente Medellín, Barcelona SC, and Colo-Colo. It was a balanced group, but Boca were the favourites. Their opening match, a hard-fought 2-1 victory against Barcelona SC, demonstrated their intent. There was no doubt that Bianchi had returned with one objective: to conquer South America once more.

Off the pitch, the expectations were unrelenting. Boca fans had not forgotten what it felt like to dominate, and now that Bianchi was back, anything less than absolute superiority was unacceptable. But *El Virrey* was never a man to be rushed. He worked in increments, refining his team match by match, ensuring that every player understood his role, that every tactical decision was executed flawlessly.

Meanwhile on the domestic front, a crucial Superclásico clash at La Bombonera carried even more weight than normal. Boca was in the hunt for the Clausura title, but so was River. A win here could tilt the scales in either direction. Having been 0-2 down at halftime, Boca hit back with a brace from Guillermo Barros Schelotto in a heated affair in which two River players received red cards.

Boca were top of the championship with just four matches left. However, with Boca also competing in the Copa Libertadores knockout rounds, Bianchi decided to prioritize the international tournament, resting key players in the final league matches. The Xeneize went past Paysandu, Cobreloa and América de Cali, which propelled the club into the Copa Libertadores finals.

Boca's domestic form dipped, allowing River to overtake them and win the Clausura. Boca would ultimately finish in second place with 39 points, four behind their arch-rivals. Bianchi had made a gamble: it was continental success or nothing. In the final, they were to face Santos.

The Brazilian side had a plethora of exciting young players, such as Diego Ribas, Renato, Alex, Nenê and a young Robinho to name but a few. They were eager to reclaim the crown last held by the club in the Pelé era. Boca, however, had absolutely no intention of letting history repeat itself at their expense.

In the first leg at La Bombonera, the atmosphere inside the stadium was powerful. The walls shook with the songs of tens of thousands of Boca faithful, their voices rising in anticipation of another historic night. Bianchi, calm and composed as always, made his way to the dugout, his mind already working through every possible scenario. The breakthrough came in the 32nd minute. A clever short corner found its way to Marcelo Delgado, whose clinical finish sent the temple into delirium.

Santos attempted to respond, but Boca's defence absorbed every attack. As the second half progressed, Boca continued to dictate the tempo, frustrating their opponents and waiting for their chance to extend the lead. That moment came in the 83rd minute. Once again, it was *Chelo* Delgado who provided the finishing touch, doubling Boca's advantage and putting them in a commanding position heading into the return leg. The final whistle confirmed what everyone in the stadium already knew: Boca had one hand on the trophy.

The return leg at São Paulo's Morumbi Stadium, presented a different challenge. Santos, playing in front of their home crowd, needed a near-miraculous performance to overturn the deficit. From the opening whistle, Boca played with the same confidence that had defined their campaign. Santos, desperate to make an early impact, threw numbers forward, but their urgency left them exposed. Boca capitalized in the 21st minute when Carlos Tevez, the young star who had come into his own during the tournament, found the back of the net with a coolly taken goal.

The hosts did not stop pushing, and in the 75th minute, Alex managed to pull one back for Santos. For a brief moment, there was hope among the Brazilian supporters, but it was short-lived. Boca, unbothered by the setback, responded with the decisiveness of a champion. Delgado, already the hero of the first leg, struck again in the 84th minute. Any lingering doubt was erased in stoppage time when Schiavi slotted away a penalty for Boca's third and final goal, putting the final nail in Santos' coffin. *El Virrey's* gamble paid off, and Boca were continental champions once again.

THIS WAS BOCA'S FIFTH Copa Libertadores title, their third in four years, an unprecedented level of dominance in modern South American football. It reaffirmed La Bombonera's status as the most feared ground on the continent. It solidified Bianchi's legacy as the greatest coach in the club's history. As the players lifted the trophy, the blue and gold confetti rained down upon them, the fans who had traveled to São Paulo erupted in song, while back in the *barrio*, the party continued for days. Boca were back in league action four days after the continental success, seeing off the final game of the Clausura, in a hugely changed squad which saw out a 7-2 defeat to Rosario Central.

The Copa Libertadores triumph meant Boca had a shot of winning another Intercontinental Cup that winter, but first the domestic Apertura championship was, for now, Bianchi's sole focus. Despite the departure of key players like Marcelo Delgado to Cruz Azul and Hugo Ibarra to Monaco, the club reinforced its squad with notable signings, including Fabián Vargas, Iarley, and Luis Perea.

The campaign commenced on August 3 2003, with an away fixture against Gimnasia. Boca secured a hard-fought 1-0 victory, signaling their intent for the season. This triumph was followed by a commanding 4-0 win over Rosario Central at a packed La Bombonera. In the Superclásico against River, the Xeneize emerged victorious with a 2-0 win at the Monumental, a result that not only boosted morale but also solidified their position as title favourites.

The championship was clinched with a victory over Arsenal at Racing's stadium in Avellaneda. Bianchi had done it again, and with games to spare. Carlitos Tevez emerged as the team's top scorer with 8 goals, while Matías Donnet contributed with his 5 goals. Now *El Virrey* could put his focus on the Intercontinental Cup, due to take place a week after Boca's final domestic game.

The opponents were European giants AC Milan, who defeated fellow Italian side Juventus in the Champions League final at Old Trafford. The *rossoneri*, led by Carlo Ancelotti, had brought an embarrassment of riches. Their lineup featured the likes of Paolo Maldini, Alessandro Nesta, Andrea Pirlo, Kaká, Gennaro Gattuso, Clarence Seedorf, and the great Andriy Shevchenko—a collection of world-class talents that many believed would overwhelm Boca's defence. But the Xeneize were absolutely no strangers of defying expectations on the world stage.

The venue was Yokohama's International Stadium, and Bianchi knew that matches like these weren't won on reputation. They were won on the pitch. Boca had arrived in Japan prepared for a war of attrition. They had studied Milan's playstyle meticulously, understanding that to win, they would need to play a near-perfect game.

The deadlock was broken in the 23rd minute when Milan's majestic midfielder Andrea Pirlo found Danish striker Jon Dahl Tomasson, who slotted the ball past Boca's goalkeeper, Roberto Abbondanzieri. Undeterred, Boca responded with renewed vigour. Just five minutes later, in the 28th minute, Matías Donnet seized upon a rebound inside the penalty area, firing a left-footed shot that leveled the score.

The remainder of regular time saw both sides creating opportunities, but neither could find the decisive goal. The match proceeded into extra time, yet the stalemate persisted, leading to the drama of a penalty shootout. Boca displayed remarkable composure, converting three of their spot-kicks, while Milan struggled, with Abbondanzieri making crucial saves. The shootout concluded 3–1 in favour of Boca, securing another Intercontinental Cup title. *El Virrey* had done it yet again.

In a record that still stands, Bianchi has now been the only manager to win this trophy on three occasions—once with Vélez and now twice with Boca. Two of these were against AC Milan: the manager had also guided his former team to success in the 1994 edition, beating Fabio Capello's *rossoneri* side.

By February 2004, Boca were back in action, as champions of Argentina, South America and the world. All eyes were on the side from the *barrio* La Boca. The Clausura and the Copa Libertadores both kicked off in the same month, and the Xeneizes had a lot to prove. The team's campaign was marked by a strong start, with notable victories against Rosario Central, Banfield, Racing, and Lanús.

Meanwhile, the club's Copa Libertadores group stage matches commenced in mid-February. Drawn into Group 8 alongside Deportivo Cali, Bolívar, and Colo-Colo, Boca faced early challenges. Their opening match, a difficult 3-1 defeat at the high altitude of La Paz against Bolívar, served as a wake-up call. However, they rebounded with a 2-0 victory over Colo-Colo at La Bombonera, followed by a crucial 1-0 away win against Deportivo Cali. The momentum continued with a commanding 3-0 home win over Deportivo Cali, solidifying their place at the top of the group. Despite a 1-0 loss to Colo-Colo in Santiago, Boca sealed their group stage campaign with a convincing 3-0 victory over Bolívar, advancing to the knockout rounds as group winners.

Back in the Clausura, Boca continued to rack up points, showing consistency despite balancing two major competitions. However, a pivotal moment occurred when Boca faced arch-rivals River at La Bombonera. Despite their efforts, Boca suffered a 1-0 defeat, a result that significantly impacted their title aspirations.

Attention quickly shifted to the Copa Libertadores knockout rounds, where Boca's reputation as a dominant force in South America was on the line. In the Round of 16, they faced Sporting Cristal from Peru. A decent aggregate win, featuring a 2-1 away victory and a 3-2 win at home, ensured their progression. The quarter-finals brought a greater challenge in the form of São Caetano from Brazil. The first leg was a stalemate at 0-0, and the second leg at La Bombonera finished 1-1. The game advanced to penalties where Boca won 4-3.

The semi finals presented the most anticipated clash of the tournament: Boca Juniors versus River Plate. A Superclásico. The first leg was held at La Bombonera on June 10, 2004. With an electric atmosphere inside the stadium, Boca took control of the match early, pressing River's defence and dictating play in midfield. In the 28th minute, Boca found the breakthrough when Rolando Schiavi broke through the River defence to head home. The roar from the Boca faithful literally shook the stadium, and River, despite their attempts to respond, failed to break through Boca's organized backline. The game ended 1-0, giving Boca a slight but significant advantage heading into the second leg.

The return leg at the Monumental was a cauldron of tension. River's stadium was packed to the brim with thousands of fans desperate to see their team overturn the deficit. The match began with Boca once again showing their defensive discipline, but River increased the pressure as the minutes ticked by. In the 51st minute, River finally found the equalizer through a goal from Lucho González, who finished a well-worked move to level the aggregate score at 1-1.

In the 87th minute, it was the young Carlos Tevez who smashed home from close range, putting Boca ahead. The young forward removed his shirt in celebration before flapping his arms like a chicken—a derogatory gesture towards their rivals. River were nicknamed by their rivals as *gallinas* (chickens), since the 1960s, in which Banfield threw a live chicken onto the pitch to taunt *los millonarios*, and somehow the nickname stuck. Boca fans were especially no strangers to use this nickname for their bitter rivals. Such weight held the gesture in the Superclásico that Tevez's action was deemed to be enough for the referee Héctor Baldassi to brandish a red card, ludicrously repeating the gesture to make sure the young forward knew why he was getting his marching orders. Tevez pleaded with the referee, completely surprised at the decision, with Guillermo Barros Schelotto looking on in anger following the jubilation.

The drama was still far from over. Five minutes into injury time, Christian Nasuti scored for River, a goal in which the Monumental nearly burst at the seams in joy. Tevez's sending off now seemed like a disaster as the game headed for a penalty shootout. Both sides converted their first four penalties each. When River's Maxi Lopez stepped up, Boca's Roberto Abbondanzieri became the hero, saving a centrally taken spot kick that was perfect for the goalkeeper to stop. When midfielder Javier Villarreal converted Boca's final penalty, the players erupted in celebration. They had eliminated their greatest rivals on their own turf, securing a place in the Copa Libertadores final in the most dramatic fashion possible.

Boca entered their fourth Libertadores final in five years facing Once Caldas, the Colombian club that had stunned the continent with their giant-killing run. The contenders had some international players in their side, such as Jhon Viáfara and Elkin Soto. They also had former Boca player Jonathan Fabbro, who years later would be sentenced to years in jail for unforgivable crimes against children.

The first leg, played at La Bombonera, ended in a frustrating 0-0 draw, a suspended Carlos Tevez meant that Boca lacked that extra bite needed to put away the chances. Travelling to Manizales, a city surrounded by mountains between Medellín and the capital Bogotá, Boca found themselves locked in another stalemate in the second leg, finishing 1-1 after extra time. The match went to penalties, and in an uncharacteristic collapse, Boca failed to score a single spot-kick. Once Caldas triumphed 2-0 in the shootout, bringing an end to Boca's reign as South American champions.

Following the shock defeat in the final, Carlos Bianchi left Boca once again. He had unquestionably been the fans' most loved manager, as evidenced by his sheer success. He would later leave Argentina for Spain, where he was employed by Atlético Madrid, but after a Copa del Rey exit, the powers that be terminated his position after only six months in the job. Years of inactivity would follow *El Virrey*.

While he is most likely the greatest Argentine manager to never coach the national team, and also while others such as César Luis Menotti and Carlos Bilardo are hailed for their World Cup triumphs, it is the domestic success of Carlos Bianchi that casts an enormously long shadow over his peers, who never brought the same level of success to Boca—or any club for that matter.

Under the new stewardship of Miguel Ángel Brindisi, one of the ex-players instrumental to Boca's 1981 title-winning side, the club sought to bring back Martín Palermo to La Boca, following his underwhelming tenure with Villareal, Real Betis and Alavés. The board felt that his experience would be the right ingredient needed for Boca alongside Carlos Tevez, who returned from the 2004 Olympics in Athens with a gold medal.

In the 2004 Recopa, Boca faced Peruvian side Cienciano, the Copa Sudamericana champions, in a single-match final at Lockhart Stadium in Fort Lauderdale. Boca took the lead with a goal from Carlos Tevez in the 33rd minute. However, Cienciano equalized dramatically in the final moments, sending the match to a penalty shootout. In the shootout, the Xeneize faltered, with Tevez and Fabián Vargas missing their penalties, leading to a 4-2 victory for Cienciano. Penalties, which had been kind in the past, would once more cause heartbreak in quick succession from the Libertadores final.

For the Apertura, along with Palermo, Boca players such as Aníbal Matellán, Ariel Carreño, and Cristian Traverso. Additionally, new signings included Claudio Morel Rodríguez, Andrés Guglielminpietro, and Ezequiel Medrán. Boca commenced the tournament with promise, but the momentum waned significantly with many losses, including a 0-2 defeat to River. This particularly troubling phase saw Boca endure a goal drought lasting 600 minutes, setting an unwanted club record in the professional era.

The team's inconsistency culminated in a mid-table finish, with 7 wins, 5 draws, and 7 losses, scoring 22 goals and conceding 16 over 19 matches. This lackluster performance led to Brindisi's resignation just three months into his tenure.

Despite domestic struggles, Boca found solace in the Copa Sudamericana, where they achieved notable success. Under interim manager Jorge "*Chino*" Benítez, embarked on a memorable campaign. Disposing of San Lorenzo and Cerro early on, the semifinals saw Boca clash with Brazilian side Internacional. A commanding 4-2 home win in the first leg set the tone, and a 0-0 draw in Porto Alegre secured their spot in the final.

In the finals, Boca faced Bolivia's Bolívar. The first leg in La Paz, with the high altitude once again being problematic, resulted in a 1-0 loss. However, in the return leg at a wedged La Bombonera, Boca triumphed 2-0, with goals from Martín Palermo and Carlos Tevez, securing the championship. Benítez now had silverware as both player and a manager.

THIS TRIUMPH MARKED Tevez's farewell appearance for Boca before his move to Corinthians. The forward went to his knees, visibly emotional and saluted the fans after his goal in the final. The cameras panned to a goateed Diego Maradona, who was celebrating with his daughter Dalma. The pictures then cut back to Tevez, hiding his tears in the Boca shirt, before walking back to his own half, raising his left arm towards *El Diego*, who raises his in return, blowing kisses.

Of course, Diego Maradona was absolutely no stranger to La Bombonera as a fan. Enjoying the religious-like adoration of his fans, he would go regularly with family and friends to his own box, with all the pizza and beer that was always available. He seemed heavier around this time, and his personal life was rarely out of the tabloids. When English striker turned TV presenter Gary Lineker travelled to Buenos Aires to meet Maradona around a year or so later for a BBC documentary, the Argentinian idol seemed thinner and happier. His natural dark, curled hair was closer to the style he sported at his 1980s peak. Maradona took Lineker to La Bombonera with the boisterous atmosphere and occasion stunning the former English striker.

CHAPTER SIXTEEN

Boca played Vélez on the 100th anniversary of the club, on April 3rd 2005. The year was dubbed the "*Xentenario*," a play on words combining "centenario" (centenary) and "xeneize". In the stadium, the club held enormous celebrations, with videos showing the story of the club on large screens and former players receiving medals. Closing the show was, of course, Diego Maradona. The celebrations were dampened as, in the game itself, Vélez beat Boca 0-2.

That year's Clausura was in fact anything to celebrate, with Boca finishing in 15th place, a disappointing outcome for the team. In the Copa Libertadores, Boca topped their group and defeated Junior in the Round of 16. However, they were eliminated in the quarterfinals by Chivas de Guadalajara, suffering a heavy 4-0 loss in the first leg. The second leg ended in controversy when "*Chino*" Benítez was involved in an incident that led to his dismissal.

The Boca coach had spat in the face of Chivas' Adolfo Bautista as he was walking off, having been sent off alongside Palermo after they had been involved in a violent altercation. Bautista left the field under police protection, but was still assaulted by a Boca fan who managed to enter the pitch. Marcelo Delgado, who the club brought back to help with the Tevez-shaped void up forward, spent the night in jail following an altercation with a police officer. The scenes descended into chaos and the Uruguayan referee Martín

Vázquez suspended play. The ugliness in La Bombonera that night put the club in bad light, especially during what was supposed to be their celebratory centenary year.

CONMEBOL suspended Palermo and Benítez, and the club received a three stadium ban. The results didn't improve. Boca didn't win any of the remaining games of the Clausura, with the final game against Almagro suspended due to both sets of crowds damaging the stadium. Both teams were deemed to have lost by a tribunal.

The following month, the club sought new leadership to restore the club's prestige, following the poor recent Clausura. Diego Maradona publicly advocated for the appointment of the charismatic and highly experienced Alfio *"Coco"* Basile as the new head coach. Responding to this endorsement and recognizing Basile's extensive experience, Boca's board appointed him as the team's manager.

Basile brought in new faces to strengthen the side. Federico Insua and *Cata* Díaz were among the first in the door. Basile wasted no time in making an impact. His first test came in the 2005 Recopa Sudamericana, where Boca, as Copa Sudamericana champions, faced Once Caldas, the reigning Copa Libertadores holders. In a tightly contested match, the Xeneize triumphed 4-3 on aggregate, securing the first title of the Basile era, who saw the victory as a statement of intent.

Focus shifted to the Apertura, and despite a loss to San Lorenzo, Boca went on a five match winning streak. The streak ended following a dull 0-0 Superclásico at the Monumental. Any championship-winning campaign is rarely a smooth ride, and Boca faced another rough patch following a shock 1-0 home defeat to Colón, which rattled the confidence of the squad, and just days later, Boca suffered a humbling 4-1 loss to Arsenal de Sarandí. It was their most humiliating performance of the season, and it threatened to derail their title charge at a crucial juncture. Doubts crept in once more, and their rivals sensed an opportunity. But champions are defined by their ability to respond under pressure.

In the matches that followed, Boca rediscovered their winning mentality. A 2-0 victory over Vélez at La Bombonera reignited belief, and a 3-1 win away to Estudiantes proved that the team had the character to grind out results when it mattered most. With just a few matches remaining, Boca was back on top, but the title was far from secured.

Gimnasia were the other team seeking to claim the silverware. Luckily they drew each of their final four fixtures, while Basile's side won theirs. After a year of frustration and setbacks, Boca had returned to their throne and won the Apertura. Celebrations in the *barrio* spilled to the centre of Buenos Aires, as *bosteros* donned flags and sang up and down the city's Avenida 9 de Julio. Rodrigo Palacio had scored 10 goals in Boca's 17 fixtures, making him the club's top scorer. A young midfielder who came from the youth ranks by the name of Fernando Gago was a standout performer during the campaign.

Boca now turned its attention to the Copa Sudamericana final against Mexico's Pumas UNAM, four days after winning the Apertura. The prospect of clinching two major titles within such a short span was a testament to the resurgence under Basile's guidance.

The club has managed to go past Cerro Porteño, Internacional and Universidad Católica en route to the final, with the first leg of the final taking place at the Estadio Olímpico Universitario in Mexico City. Boca and UNAM battled to a 1-1 draw, setting up a thrilling conclusion in the Argentinian capital.

The return leg at La Bombonera, was a spectacle of footballing drama. Both teams once again finished 1-1 after regular time, mirroring the first leg's scoreline. The championship would be decided by yet another penalty shootout. In this high-pressure scenario, Boca's goalkeeper, Roberto Abbondanzieri, emerged as the hero. He not only saved two penalties but also converted the decisive spot-kick himself, leading Boca to a dramatic 4-3 victory in the shootout. The centenary year started terribly, but now under the great *Coco* Basile, Boca clinched three titles in a matter of months, an incredible end of the club's *Xentenario*.

With no time to rest on their laurels, Boca entered the 2006 Clausura with full focus on it. The team got off to a rocky start when they faced Gimnasia with the match ending in a 2-1 defeat. However, this setback was short-lived. Boca rebounded with a hard-fought 2-1 victory against Rosario Central.

Boca played fantastic in the weeks that followed. The much-anticipated Superclásico against River on matchday 11, ended in a very lucky 1-1 draw, a game in which Boca were down to nine men. But football is a results business, and this result maintained Boca's lead in the standings.

By this time Guillermo Barros Schelotto was being used less frequently by Basile. The Superclásico turned out to be his last time wearing the famous *azul y oro,* with younger, sharper players such as Palacio taking his place in the starting eleven. The 33-year-old left Boca for the United States, when he joined Columbus Crew in the MLS.

Boca went unbeaten for the rest of the season. They wrapped up the Clausura championship away to Independiente in the penultimate game of the season. The campaign concluded with a 2-0 home win against Olimpo, adding an exclamation point to a remarkable campaign. Defensively, the team was resolute, conceding only 12 goals in 19 matches, while the attacking partnership of Rodrigo Palacio and Martín Palermo—known as *Pa-Pa*—instilled fear in the defences of opposing teams. "*Boca bicampeon,*" read the newspapers, as Basile achieved his fourth consecutive title for the Xeneize, an unprecedented record for a manager of the famous club from La Boca.

Basile's success enabled Boca fans to transform Buenos Aires into a sea of blue and gold, parading through La Boca with flags, fireworks, and relentless chants with the percussive sounds synonymous with the club. Nowhere else do supporters create such an intimidating yet electrifying ambiance, making the club's culture an emotional, chaotic, and beautiful force that remains unmatched worldwide.

Argentina's 2006 World Cup campaign was filled with promise but ended in heartbreak. Under José Pekerman, they played beautiful, attacking football, topping their group and famously thrashing Serbia 6-0. After defeating Mexico in extra time, courtesy of one of the finest volleys in the competition's history thanks to Maxi Rodríguez, the *albiceleste* faced hosts Germany in the quarterfinals. Leading 1-0, Pekerman controversially substituted Riquelme, and Argentina conceded, eventually losing on penalties. The defeat was crushing, and Pekerman left the position, AFA appointed "*Coco*" Basile, who had previously led Argentina to two Copa América titles in the '90s.

Boca's club president, Mauricio Macri, had negotiated with AFA so that Basile could stay on as manager until after the 2006 Recopa. As 2005 Copa Sudamericana champions, Boca faced 2005 Copa Libertadores winners São Paulo, who were led by their unusually prolific goal-scoring goalkeeper, Rogério Ceni.

The first leg, played at La Bombonera saw Boca overpower the Brazilian giants with a commanding 2-1 victory. São Paulo went ahead on the half hour mark, courtesy of Thiago Ribeiro, but the home side pulled two back thanks to Rodrigo Palacio's keen eye for goal. Boca would go into the second leg with the advantage.

The second leg, held at the Morumbi Stadium, was a tense battle, with São Paulo pushing hard to overturn the deficit. However, Boca's spirit shone through. Palacio and Palermo struck again, silencing the home crowd, and while São Paulo responded with an equalizer, they couldn't find the late goal to put them back into the game. Boca won 4-3 on aggregate and "*Coco*" Basile won his fifth title in 425 days.

Boca began the 2006 Apertura like true champions, playing with confidence and fluidity. The squad was stacked with experienced legends and rising stars—led by Martín Palermo, Rodrigo Palacio, Fernando Gago, and Hugo Ibarra—each playing a key role. Ricardo La Volpe, a former goalkeeper of San Lorenzo who was part of Argentina's 1978 World Cup winning squad, took over the managerial reins.

La Volpe wasn't the club's first choice. Marcelo Bielsa and Miguel Ángel Russo were the two names the board insisted on before finally turning to the former Mexico national team coach. In his first game, in a goalless draw against Godoy Cruz, La Volpe enraged some fans by wearing a red tie—the colour famously associated with bitter rivals River.

Boca travelled across town for the Superclásico, in which River won 3-1, ending a 22-match unbeaten run, but seven wins and a draw over the next eight games put the club in serious contention for the championship, with only Estudiantes catching up with them. A victory against Belgrano would mean they would seal the title, but Boca lost the encounter unexpectedly 1-0. The title would go down to the final day. But a 2-1 home defeat to Lanús, which stunned both players and supporters. These consecutive losses left Boca level on points with Estudiantes, necessitating a championship playoff to determine the Apertura winner.

Boca met Estudiantes a little under a fortnight before Christmas at the Estadio José Amalfitani. It started well, with the reliable Martín Palermo putting the Xeneizes 1-0 up after four minutes. However, in the second half, Diego Simeone's Estudiantes side showed immense resilience and turned the match around.

The turning point came when José Sosa equalized, shifting momentum completely. Estudiantes continued pressing, and ten minutes before the end, Mariano Pavone, a *bostero* who was once a youth player at Boca until he was 14, delivered the final blow, scoring the winning goal that sealed Estudiantes' dramatic 2-1 victory. Boca players were left stunned, and La Volpe resigned immediately after the match, taking responsibility for the failure.

Six months previously, Miguel Ángel Russo had agreed to stay on as Vélez manager. Two days after the heartbreaking tie against Estudiantes, the Boca board got their man, as he filled the vacant role. He was joined by the return of a club icon, Juan Román Riquelme.

After leaving Boca for Barcelona in 2002, Riquelme struggled to adapt to European football. Despite his immense talent, he clashed with Barça coach Louis van Gaal, who did not see him as a key player, often playing him out of his best position. In 2003, he was loaned to Villarreal, where he was utilized more frequently, leading them to the 2006 Champions League semi finals, the greatest achievement in their history at that point. His peers in Spain could recognize his brilliance, so much so that when Zinedine Zidane played his final ever club game, it was with Riquelme who he swapped jerseys with at full time at the French maestro's request.

However, by early 2007, his relationship with Villarreal coach Manuel Pellegrini deteriorated. After missing a crucial penalty against Arsenal in that semifinal, Riquelme was somewhat deemed surplus to requirements by the Chilean coach. Had Villareal made the final, they would have faced Barcelona which would have been the perfect moment for revenge for the player to get his revenge on the club that were more than happy to let him go some years prior. Riquelme was frozen out of the Villareal squad. The player, frustrated by his lack of game time, knew that he had to leave in order to play regularly. This triggered alarm bells back in Buenos Aires, prompting Boca to try to negotiate a loan deal to bring him back.

Boca president Mauricio Macri worked tirelessly to negotiate a deal with Villarreal. Since Boca could not afford to buy Riquelme outright, they secured a six-month loan deal, with the Spanish side agreeing to cover most of his wages. In January 2007, the deal was made and Boca's idol was making his return.

The moment Riquelme stepped back onto the familiar pitch at La Bombonera, Boca transformed into a different team. His incredible vision, precise passing, and intelligence immediately elevated the team's play, giving them the creative spark they had lacked. In the Copa Libertadores, he was untouchable.

BOCA JUNIORS WERE DRAWN into Group 7 alongside Mexico's Toluca, Peru's Cienciano, and Bolivia's Bolívar. The group stage presented a series of challenges, testing the team's strengths and adaptability. The campaign commenced with an away fixture against Bolívar in La Paz. The high altitude once again posed significant challenges, and the tie ended goalless. Hosting Cienciano at La Bombonera, Boca showcased their attacking ferocity. A goal from Ibarra secured a 1-0 victory, reinstating confidence within the squad.

Boca traveled to Mexico to face Toluca, where they succumbed to a 2-0 loss. The return fixture in Buenos Aires saw Boca dominate possession in an emphatic 3-0 victory for the Xeneizes. Facing Cienciano in Cusco, Boca endured a 3-0 defeat. The loss highlighted defensive frailties and the challenges of yet again playing at high altitudes. Needing a decisive victory to progress, Boca hosted Bolívar. Rising to the occasion, they delivered a commanding performance, winning 7-0. This emphatic win secured Boca's passage to the knockout stages as group runners-up.

Advancing to the Round of 16, Boca faced fellow Argentine side Vélez Sársfield. The tie was anticipated to be a tactical battle, given the familiarity between the teams. Up stepped Riquelme who inspired the Xeneize to a 3-0 win, himself opening the scoring with a wonderfully curled shot into the top corner. The return fixture at Estadio José Amalfitani saw Vélez secure a 3-1 win. However, Boca's away goal, courtesy of a Riquelme *gol olímpico*, meaning a goal scored directly from a corner, ensured their progression on aggregate.

Hosting Libertad, Boca faced a formidable opponent. The match concluded in a 1-1 draw, with Palermo scoring a crucial last-minute equalizer. Travelling to Asunción, Boca delivered a masterclass in tactical discipline. Goals from Riquelme and Palacio secured a 2-0 victory, sending Boca into the last four.

The semifinal clash pitted Boca against Colombia's Cúcuta Deportivo, a team that had been the tournament's surprise package. In San Cristóbal, the side from La Boca struggled to adapt to the humid conditions and artificial turf, resulting in a 3-1 defeat. Ledesma's away goal provided a glimmer of hope for the return leg.

Amidst a foggy night in the Argentinian capital, Boca produced a memorable performance at La Bombonera. Riquelme orchestrated the midfield, scoring a sublime free-kick to open the scoring. The fog was so thick by the time Boca scored their second goal courtesy of Palermo, *bosteros* behind the goal at the other end of the pitch couldn't actually see it and just heard the roar of the crowd at the opposite end. A Sebastián Battaglia header six minutes from the end secured a 3-0 win, overturning the deficit and booking a place in the final.

It was an Argentina-Brazil rivalry for the two-legged affair, as Boca were to face Grêmio. The match commenced with Grêmio pressing high, attempting to unsettle Boca's defence. However, Boca's experience and tactical discipline allowed them to weather the early pressure. In the 18th minute, Boca broke the deadlock. A well-executed set-piece saw Riquelme deliver a precise free-kick into the box. Martín Palermo connected with a cross, directing it towards goal, and Rodrigo Palacio, positioned advantageously, tapped it in to give Boca the lead.

Grêmio's efforts to equalize were hampered by Boca's cohesive defensive structure. The Argentine side controlled the midfield, with Riquelme orchestrating play and dictating the tempo. As the match progressed, Grêmio's frustration became evident, leading to a pivotal moment in the 57th minute when Sandro Goiano received a red card for a reckless two-footed challenge on the torso of Éver Banega, reducing the Brazilian side to ten men.

Seizing the numerical advantage, Boca intensified their attacks. In the 73rd minute, Riquelme showcased his set-piece speciality by curling a sublime free-kick past goalkeeper Sebastián Saja to double Boca's lead. La Bombonera absolutely erupted. *La avalancha* engulfing everyone and everything in its path behind the goal.

The final blow came in the 89th minute. Riquelme, displaying his dribbling skills, maneuvered past Grêmio's defenders and unleashed a shot from outside the box. Saja managed a partial save, the ball then came back out of the area. Palermo picked it up and sent in a cross to Ledesma, who headed it skyward, Dátolo went in to challenge, and it bounced off Patricio and into the net, resulting in an own goal and sealing a 3–0 victory for Boca.

The return leg occurred in Porto Alegre at the Estádio Olímpico Monumental, a grand bowl of a stadium for 45,000 spectators. Facing a daunting three-goal deficit, Grêmio needed an extraordinary performance to overturn the aggregate score. From the outset, Grêmio displayed urgency, pushing forward in search of an early goal. Despite their endeavors, clear-cut chances were scarce, with Boca's defence remaining resolute. The first half saw the Brazilian side come close, with an effort striking the post, but the breakthrough eluded them.

The second half saw former Boca player Rolando Schiavi hit the post, but in the 68th minute. Riquelme, once again at the heart of Boca's offense, received the ball outside the penalty area and unleashed a powerful shot that found the back of the net, effectively ending Grêmio's hopes of a comeback. Eight minutes later, Boca struck again. A swift counter-attack saw Rodrigo Palacio's shot parried by Saja, only for Riquelme to pounce on the rebound and slot it home, securing a 2–0 victory on the night and a 5–0 aggregate triumph.

Boca were champions of South America again. Libertadores number six was being celebrated back in Buenos Aires as the fireworks were being set alight, as fans and *porteños* looked at the night sky that once again illuminated with familiar blue and yellow colours. Back in the *barrio*, residents and fans poured into the streets, their voices harmonizing in chants and songs that echoed throughout the night. The air was thick with the aroma of traditional Argentine *asado*, as impromptu barbecues sprang up, washed down with plenty of *fernet con coca*.

Juan Román Riquelme's influence throughout the finals was undeniable. His vision, technical ability, and composure under pressure earned him the Man of the Match award in both legs. Not only that, he was the tournament's best player and by some considerable distance. Following the conclusion of his loan spell, he returned to Villarreal, and Boca were without their star player for the Apertura, which ran from August to December.

Over in Spain, his relationship with the club had very much deteriorated, leading to zero playing opportunities under Manuel Pellegrini. Despite training with the squad, Riquelme was not included in matchday selections. Boca felt that a player of his calibre didn't belong on the sidelines, and they could really do with him, as evidenced by their domestic campaign. Without Riquelme, Boca finished fourth as Lanús won their first ever championship.

Riquelme was also absent for the 2007 FIFA Club World Cup, where Boca Juniors represented South America as the reigning Copa Libertadores champions.Entering the competition at the semi-final stage, they faced Tunisia's Étoile SS, securing a narrow 1-0 victory to advance to the final. In the final held a week before Christmas, at Yokohama's International Stadium, Boca were faced against Italy's AC Milan—the same venue and the same team who the Xeneize met four years before. Despite a decent effort, the club were defeated 4-2. Palacio and Ledesma scored for Boca, while Milan's goals came from Filippo Inzaghi with two, as well as Alessandro Nesta, and the *rossoneri's* maestro Kaká.

By now, Mauricio Macri concluded his presidency at Boca, paving the way for Pedro Pompilio to assume the role. This transition allowed Macri to channel his focus towards a political career. He founded the political party Commitment for Change (CPC) in 2003, which later evolved into the Republican Proposal (PRO). While many had said that Macri was using Boca to launch a political career, one could be forgiven for being skeptical as his political journey saw him serve as Chief of Government of Buenos Aires, followed by his election as President of Argentina, a position he held from 2015 to 2019. Macri's centre-right political stance was, for many, always at odds with Boca's working-class roots.

CHAPTER
SEVENTEEN

In the 2008 Clausura, Boca embarked on a campaign under new manager Carlos Ischia, who had previously served as assistant to the esteemed Carlos Bianchi. Ischia was also a former player, who spent a number of years at Vélez, alongside *El Virrey*. As his number two, Ischia was familiar with Boca, the staff and the players. The club also welcomed back playmaker Juan Román Riquelme, whose return was a beacon of hope for the Xeneizes, igniting aspirations of reclaiming domestic glory. He signed a highly lucrative deal with Boca on a permanent deal, making him the most paid player in the history of the game in Argentina.

Boca won their first four games in a row. The 1-0 home triumph over arch-rivals River mid-way through the campaign, excited fans as Riquelme's strategic brilliance was on full display. Throughout the tournament, Boca demonstrated fortitude, suffering only two defeats: a 1-0 loss to San Lorenzo on and a 1-0 setback against Estudiantes. The team concluded the Clausura with an emphatic 6-2 victory over Tigre. But it wasn't enough as it was River who finished on top of the league, four points ahead of the Xeneize.

The following Apertura coincided with an increasing digital revolution, enabling fans worldwide to follow matches through emerging internet streaming platforms, both legal and illegal. This technological shift allowed expatriates and international supporters to experience the fervor of La Bombonera from afar, strengthening Boca's global community.

Boca's campaign commenced with a commanding 4-0 victory over Gimnasia de Jujuy at La Bombonera. However, the journey was anything but smooth. The team encountered unexpected defeats, such as a 3-2 loss to Tigre and a 4-1 setback against Godoy Cruz Despite these hurdles, Boca showcased their mettle by securing crucial victories, notably a 1-0 win against arch-rivals River Plate at the Monumental.

Tragedy struck when Pedro Pompilio, president of the club and less than a year into the job, died unexpectedly of a heart attack on October 30, 2008, at age 58. His passing led to Jorge Amor Ameal, then vice president, assuming the presidency.

The Apertura concluded with Boca, Tigre, and San Lorenzo deadlocked at 39 points each, necessitating a rare three-way playoff to determine the champion. In this triangular series, Boca defeated San Lorenzo 3-1 on December 20 but fell 1-0 to Tigre on December 23. Nevertheless, Boca's superior goal difference in the playoff secured them the championship.

The playoff format added a layer of excitement and unpredictability to the race, captivating fans nationwide–and thanks to the internet, also worldwide. This victory marked Boca's 23rd professional league title. But for many fans, the victory was much, much sweeter with rivals River finishing right at the bottom of the table. Months after clinching the Clausura title, the team experienced a ridiculous decline, concluding the Apertura with only two wins, eight draws, and nine losses, totaling a mere 14 points.

Expectations were high as the squad embarked on the 2009 Clausura tournament and the prestigious Copa Libertadores campaign. However, the team's form wavered, leading to early exits and disappointing league standings. This downturn culminated in Ischia's departure in mid-2009, prompting the club to seek a seasoned tactician to restore its fortunes.

The summer had marked the return of Alfio "*Coco*" Basile to the club. Having previously led the team to success, Basile's reappointment was met with optimism. His inaugural assignment was the Audi Cup in Germany, a friendly tournament featuring European heavyweights Manchester United, Bayern Munich, and AC Milan. Having been beaten by the English side in the opening game, Boca concluded the tournament by beating Milan on penalties in the third-place playoff, their second game in as many days.

For the Apertura, key departures included Fabián Vargas, Luciano Figueroa, and long-time stalwart Rodrigo Palacio. To bolster the squad, Boca acquired Chilean midfielder Gary Medel and Uruguayan defender Adrián Gunino. Additionally, familiar faces like Federico Insúa, Guillermo Marino, and Ariel Rosada returned to La Bombonera, aiming to inject experience and creativity into the lineup.

The season was marked with inconsistencies. They exited the Copa Sudamericana at the first hurdle, and the performances of the team are very poor, miles away from the previous Apertura. "*Coco*" Basile couldn't repeat the successes a few years prior. Not ideal given that far more eyes were watching these performances live, as the nationalization of football broadcasting rights led to the "*Fútbol para Todos*" program, which made matches far more accessible to a broader audience. Following the resignation of Basile, it became a year of introspection for the club. Amid managerial changes, inconsistent performances, to the backdrop of a shifting cultural landscape, Boca faced challenges that tested its adaptability.

But sadly the slump spilled into 2010. Boca had no continental campaign, so its sole focus would be on trying to earn some domestic achievements. But it wasn't to be. The club finished 16th, their worst in a couple of decades, securing only five wins, five draws, and enduring nine losses. They scored 28 goals and conceded 35, resulting in a goal difference of -7. Martín Palermo was a standout performer, netting ten goals in 19 appearances. He then became Boca's all-time leading scorer, surpassing Roberto Cherro's record, which he held for over 70 years. For his record breaking 219th goal for the club, one player walked in the opposite direction as the players were celebrating: Riquelme. The pair's relationship at this point was fractured beyond repair for reasons unknown.

The season's instability led to managerial changes. Abel Alves resigned after a series of poor results, and Roberto Pompei took over as interim coach, achieving a balance of three wins and three losses.

That year's Apertura was another disappointing campaign for Boca, reflecting ongoing instability within the club. Under Claudio Borghi, who took over as manager, Boca failed to find consistency. The season began with promise but quickly unraveled, with defensive frailties and a lack of coordination plaguing the team. Boca finished 12th, winning just six of their 19 matches, drawing four, and losing nine.

Borghi resigned in November after a string of poor results, and Roberto Pompei once again stepped in as interim coach. Sadly it was to be an otherwise frustrating campaign. Palermo, in his final full season, scored six goals, but Boca's overall attacking play lacked fluidity. The club's struggles throughout 2010 made it clear that major changes were needed to return to title contention. By the end of the year, Boca was preparing for a fresh start.

Under manager Julio César Falcioni, Boca entered the Clausura with hopes of rebuilding after several disappointing campaigns. The team started inconsistently, struggling to find attacking rhythm despite boasting veteran stars like Juan Román Riquelme and Martín Palermo, who was playing his final professional season. He played his final game in a 2-2 draw against Gimnasia, the end of an enormous career in the famous *azul y oro*. He retired as an icon in the hearts of Boca fans.

Meanwhile, the defining moment of the season came in June, when River—Boca's eternal rivals—suffered the humiliation of relegation to the second division for the first time in their 110-year history. The warning signs had been there for years. Argentina's relegation system, which calculates an average of points over three seasons, had put River in danger due to poor performances in 2008-09 and 2009-10. But still, few believed the unthinkable could happen. As the 2010-11 season unfolded, River's struggles deepened, and their fate was sealed when they finished in a relegation playoff against Belgrano de Córdoba, a team hungry to make history. A 2-0 loss in the first leg and a tense 1-1 draw at the Monumental sealed their fate, sending shockwaves across world football.

Boca fans immediately took to the streets in celebration, waving banners that read *"Yo te vi descender"* ("I saw you go down"). New songs were composed overnight, mocking their fallen rivals. But perhaps the most enduring nickname Boca fans gave River was *"El Fantasma de la B"*—the Phantom of the B—forever branding them as the ghost of Argentina's second division. But the most famous tribute to River's humiliation came in the form of a new chant that would echo in stadiums for years to come:

"River, decime qué se siente, haber jugado el Nacional..."

("River, tell me how it feels, to having played the Nacional...")

From that day, many stopped calling the Boca—River fixture as Superclásico. It's now just "clásico". The word *super* is no longer needed as no team who has ever played in the B can be involved in a fixture with this word. This isn't technically true, but there's a great section of *bosteros* who will tell you this.

For Boca, the 2011 Apertura would always be strange with River playing in the Nacional B. Julio César Falcioni, renowned for his defensive acumen, was appointed to steer the ship. Recognizing the need for experience and stability, Falcioni bolstered the squad with key signings: goalkeeper Agustín Orión, defender Rolando Schiavi returning to the fold, and forward Darío Cvitanich.

Throughout the Apertura, the team conceded a mere six goals over 19 matches—a record in short tournaments. The defensive lineup, featuring Orión between the posts, flanked by Roncaglia, Schiavi, Insaurralde, and Clemente Rodríguez, formed a tight unit at the back. This defensive perseverence laid the foundation for Boca's unbeaten streak during the competition.

The defining moment arrived when Boca faced Banfield at La Bombonera. A comprehensive 3–0 victory, featuring a brace from Cvitanich against his former club, clinched the title with two games to spare. The atmosphere was chaotic, as fans celebrated the end of a three-year title drought.

Boca Juniors returned to the Copa Libertadores in 2012 after a period of absence, following their undefeated domestic championship. Their campaign commenced on February 14, 2012, with a goalless draw against Venezuelan side Zamora.

This match highlighted underlying tensions between star player Riquelme and coach Julio César Falcioni. Riquelme, known for his creative and attacking style, often found Falcioni's defensive tactics limiting, leading to huge dressing-room disagreements, that included the manager threatening to hand in his resignation on the plane back to Argentina. Eventually a truce was made, but the pair's relationship felt like something of a ticking time-bomb.

In the Round of 16, Boca faced Chilean side Unión Española. The first leg at La Bombonera resulted in a 2–1 victory, with goals from Riquelme and Santiago Silva. In the return leg in Santiago, Boca secured a 3–2 win, with Riquelme playing a pivotal role by scoring once and assisting two goals, thus advancing with a 5–3 aggregate.

The quarter-finals saw Boca pitted against Brazil's Fluminense. The first leg in Buenos Aires saw Boca clinch a narrow 1–0 win, courtesy of a goal set up by Riquelme. The second leg in Rio de Janeiro ended in a 1–1 draw, with Boca's goal coming late in the match, ensuring their progression to the semifinals with a 2–1 aggregate score.

The semi finals brought Boca face-to-face with Universidad de Chile. The first leg at home was a commanding 2–0 victory for Boca, setting a strong precedent. The return leg in Santiago concluded in a 0–0 draw, a result that secured Boca's place in the finals.

The two-legged final was a highly anticipated clash against Brazil's Corinthians. The first leg at La Bombonera ended in a 1–1 draw, with Boca initially taking the lead before Corinthians equalized late in the game. The decisive second leg in São Paulo saw Corinthians secure a heartbreaking 2–0 victory, courtesy of two goals from the *Timão*'s Qatari-capped, Brazilian-born striker Emerson Sheik.

Following Boca's defeat, Juan Román Riquelme announced his departure from the club. Citing feelings of exhaustion and an inability to contribute further, Riquelme stated he felt "empty" and had nothing more to give to the team. This announcement led to widespread speculation about his future, with various clubs expressing interest in acquiring his services. Despite the numerous offers, Riquelme remained inactive for several months, taking time to reflect on his career and future prospects.

AFA, at this time, had implemented significant changes to its top-tier league structure. The traditional Aperture and Clausura tournaments, which had each crowned separate champions annually since 1991, were rebranded as Torneo Inicial ("Initial Tournament") and Torneo Final ("Final Tournament"). This rebranding aimed to modernize the league's image and align its structure more closely with international standards.

Under the new format, both the Torneo Inicial and Torneo Final continued as separate competitions within a single season, each involving all participating teams playing against one another. However, unlike the previous system where each tournament's winner was declared national champion, AFA introduced a decisive match between the winners of the Inicial and Final tournaments. This championship final determined the overall Argentine champion for that season.

Boca began the Inicial with a 3–0 defeat to Quilmes, but the team quickly rebounded, securing four consecutive victories against Tigre, All Boys, Unión de Santa Fe, and Atlético Rafaela. River were back in the top flight, following a season in the second tier. The fixture at the Monumental was marred by violent incidents that underscored the intense rivalry between the two clubs. The match, which ended in a 2–2 draw, was overshadowed by clashes between fans, both inside and outside the stadium. These altercations led to injuries and arrests, highlighting the persistent issue of football-related violence in Argentina. Throughout the tournament, Boca recorded nine wins, six draws, and four losses, scoring 25 goals and conceding 20.

Juan Román Riquelme, now inactive, had been by now the subject of widespread transfer speculation, with clubs from various countries expressing interest in the playmaker. There were rumors linking him to Australia's A-League clubs, including Melbourne Heart and Western Sydney Wanderers. However, his agent Daniel Bolotnicoff, refuted these claims, stating that no Australian club had made formal contact regarding his client.

Carlos Bianchi, the club's most successful manager, returned to the club for a third tenure, just before Christmas 2012, following the non-renewal of Julio César Falcioni's contract. Riquelme emerged from his seven month break from football to don the *azul y oro* once more in time for the Torneo Final in 2013.

The optimistic supporters soon had broken hearts, as the previous glories commanded by *El Virrey* were not to be. At one point, the team endured a 12-match winless streak, setting an unfortunate club record. Defensive frailties were evident, with Boca conceding 29 goals—an average of 1.53 per game—while scoring only 13 times, averaging 0.68 goals per match. Defeats included a ludicrous 1–6 loss to San Martín, a 0–3 away defeat against San Lorenzo, and a 0–4 away loss to Newell's, the eventual champions.

Despite domestic challenges, Boca displayed bravery in the 2013 Copa Libertadores. They advanced from the group stage, only to seek perfect revenge by eliminating defending champions Corinthians in the Round of 16, with Riquelme becoming the club's top scorer in the competition's history, netting his 25th goal.

The journey sadly concluded in the quarter finals, where they were ousted by Newell's Old Boys after a dramatic penalty shootout that ended 10–9.

The poor campaign led to an enormous amount of restructuring, with over a dozen players being shifted out. To bolster the squad, the club acquired Daniel Díaz, Emanuel Insúa, the return of Fernando Gago, Jesús Méndez, Franco Cángele, Emmanuel Gigliotti, Emanuel Trípodi, and Claudio Riaño. It was clear the club needed a substantial overhaul.

Throughout the tournament, Boca maintained proximity to the top positions but couldn't quite seize the lead decisively. A notable highlight was their victory in the Superclásico, where Emmanuel Gigliotti scored the solitary goal at the Monumental, marking Boca's first win at that venue since 2008. Despite such moments, inconsistency plagued their campaign; they secured eight wins, five draws, and suffered six losses, culminating in a total of 29 points and a seventh-place finish. Riquelme, now seemingly past his peak, only made twelve appearances, with two goals. Emmanuel Gigliotti emerged as a key player, leading the team's scoring chart with eight goals. Despite the team's efforts, the team supported by the new Argentinian-born Pope Francis, San Lorenzo, clinched the championship with 33 points, leaving Boca to reflect on a season of near-misses and the need for far greater consistency in future campaigns.

Boca went into the early stages of the 2014 Torneo Final struggling to find consistency in their performances. Despite the rocky start, Boca managed to secure crucial victories, including a 2-0 win over Olimpo and a 2-1 triumph against Racing. During the Superclásico against River at La Bombonera. Despite a goal from Riquelme, Boca suffered a 2-1 defeat, with River's Ramiro Funes

Mori scoring a late winner. This loss marked River's first victory at Boca's home ground in a decade and was a significant setback for Boca's title aspirations.

In the penultimate game, Riquelme played for the last time in a Boca jersey. In the 88th minute, Riquelme was substituted off the field, receiving a standing ovation from the Boca supporters. The cameras pan to supporters, one of the flags, all of them saddened by the inevitable end of this giant of a player at the club. One of the flags read "*Boca es mi templo. Román es mi Dios. Azul y oro mi religión*" ('Boca is my temple. Román is my God. Blue and gold my religion'). It summed up the feelings *bosteros* had for him; godlike. He made 206 appearances at La Bombonera, more than any player before him.

Riquelme departed Boca to join the club where it started for him, Argentinos Juniors, where he spent six months. He would later almost sign for Cerro in Paraguay, on a record-breaking salary for football in the country. But ultimately called time on his illustrious career before his signature touched the contract.

The club finished the Final well, but it wasn't enough as the league title went across town to rivals River, just three years after their humiliating relegation. While Boca showcased moments of brilliance and mounted a late challenge for the title, inconsistency in the early stages and key defeats hindered their championship ambitions. The club were now looking to the future without their star *enganche*.

Argentina made the final of the World Cup in 2014 in a repeat fixture of the classic 1986 and 1990 finals, against Germany. The European side once again defeated Argentina 1-0 in the Maracanã Stadium in Rio, with Mario Götze scoring the winning goal in extra time. The *Albiceleste*, led by Lionel Messi, arguably the greatest player in the world at this point, fell short.

AFA introduced a transitional tournament, the Torneo de Transición, as a precursor to the expansion of the Primera División to 30 teams the following year. The Transición commenced the following month, with Boca suffering a 0-1 home defeat to Newell's. This loss was indicative of the team's inconsistent form under coach Carlos Bianchi. After a series of underwhelming performances, Bianchi was relieved of his duties. Despite a disappointing third coming, *El Virrey* remains the club's most successful manager and is held in the highest regard among Boca fans to this day. Everyone wanted the manager to do well, but some things simply aren't meant to be. As president of the club, Daniel Angelici had to make the decision. The team needed fresh guidance. A day after his departure in the La Bombonera dugout, former player Rodolfo Arruabarrena was appointed as the new head coach.

El Vasco Arruabarrena left Boca as a player in 2000, joining Villareal among a number of Xeneize players to make the trip to the small Spanish town. He also spent a season in Greece with AEK, playing alongside Rivaldo, before returning back to Argentina to join Tigre. After a single championship-winning season with Universidad in Chile, the left-back hung up his boots. He entered management, firstly with Tigre, and then secondly with Nacional, across the Río de la Plata in Uruguay.

For him, replacing his former manager, who was synonymous with some of Boca's finest years, *El Vasco* knew he'd have to give it his all. Club president Daniel Angelici knew this also. The club elections were due the following year, and getting this appointment wrong could mean his being voted out of power at La Boca. Angelici initially wanted Guillermo Barros Schelotto for the role, having performed admirably as Lanús' manager, but it wasn't possible for him at that particular time. Ricardo Lunari was rumoured to be the back-up plan if Arruabarrena wasn't appointed.

Under El Vasco, Boca did improve. The club lost three of the first four games under Bianchi. They lost the same amount from the remaining fifteen games. As the season was coming towards its conclusion, Boca advanced to the semifinals of the Copa Sudamericana, where they faced River. The first leg at La Bombonera ended in a goalless draw, but Boca was edged out 0-1 in the return leg at El Monumental. River went on to win their first continental title in seventeen years. While the domestic campaign showcased moments of promise under Arruabarrena, the inability to maintain consistent form prevented Boca from mounting a serious title challenge. Racing won the title, ending a thirteen year drought.

In 2015, ten teams from the Nacional B were promoted. There were now 30 teams in the league. Boca went the first twelve games unbeaten under Arruabarrena. At this time, the club had to face rivals River three times in the space of ten days. The league game was a well earned 2-0 victory at La Bombonera. The second was when the two sides met in the last 16 of the Copa Libertadores–the first time the two sides met in continental competition in over a decade. At the game at the Monumental, River secured a narrow 1-0 victory courtesy of a dubious penalty, which was converted by Uruguayan Diego Sánchez.

For the return leg at La Bombonera, the tension was already at an all-time high, given the number of Superclásicos in the past week or so. The first half was a tense, physical encounter, ending in a goalless draw. Boca had more possession but struggled to break down River's disciplined back four. However, it was during half-time that the night took a dark turn.

As River's players walked out of the tunnel for the second half, they were suddenly attacked with a burning chemical substance, later identified as pepper spray or homemade acid, thrown by a supporter with links to Boca's *barra brava*. The toxic fumes engulfed several players, including Leonardo Ponzio, Matías Kranevitter, Ramiro Funes Mori, and Leonel Vangioni, who were seen wiping their eyes, struggling to breathe, and collapsing on the pitch. The match was stopped immediately as chaos unfolded. Boca's players remained on the field, waiting for a decision, while River's squad, suffering from severe irritation in their eyes and skin, refused to return.

After half an hour had passed, CONMEBOL officials, referees, and security discussed the situation. The crowd at La Bombonera continued chanting, unsure of what would happen next. Some *bosteros* were throwing objects at the River contingent. After fifty minutes of delay, the match was officially suspended. River's players were escorted off the field under police protection while objects rained down from the stands. The following days were filled with uncertainty, but ultimately, CONMEBOL ruled in favour of *los millonarios*, thus eliminating Boca from the tournament. Boca was also fined and sanctioned for the incident. The incident brought criticism upon Boca's management and led to increased security measures at the stadium. The club found the supporter responsible, and banned him from La Bombonera for life. River went on to win the tournament.

Carlos Tevez, the one-time heir apparent to Diego Maradona, left Boca in 2005 for Brazilian side Corinthians, where he won a league title. He left in a controversial transfer alongside team-mate and former River defender, Javier Mascherano for West Ham the following year. Following a lengthy loan spell at Manchester United with a huge amount of silverware, Tevez joined their bitter rivals Manchester City on a permanent transfer in 2009. City had historically been mostly in the shadows of the success of their neighbours. In the late 2000's, the cash being injected into the club from foreign investment, brought elite players and, with it, a significant amount of success for the blue half of the city. Tevez was central to their on-pitch success. In 2013, he joined Juventus, where he helped the club win two Serie A titles, the Coppa Italia, and reach the 2015 Champions League final, where they were defeated by Barcelona.

Despite still being one of the best forwards in the world, he decided to return to Argentina, rejecting offers from top European clubs and lucrative contracts from other leagues. He agreed to rejoin Boca, and when his decision was seen as a rare case of a player prioritizing love for his childhood club over financial gain. When the move was confirmed, *bosteros* celebrated in the streets, and the club held an official presentation at La Bombonera, where thousands of supporters filled the stadium to welcome him back.

Days later, Tevez immediately became the leader of Boca's attack in his debut against Quilmes. Boca won the game 2-1, with their winning goal courtesy of an absolutely world-class rabona from young striker Jonathan Calleri, nephew of former Boca defender Néstor Fabbri, which inch-perfectly chipped the goalkeeper. The stadium, however, sang Carlitos' name throughout the 90 minutes. His presence on the pitch was felt right away, bringing experience, skill, and an unmatched winning mentality.

Boca's domestic campaign was characterized by a series of impressive performances. The team secured crucial victories against formidable opponents, including a notable win over arch-rivals River, which bolstered their position at the top of the league table.

Despite occasional setbacks, Boca's consistency was evident throughout the season.

The culmination of their efforts came when Boca clinched the Primera División title, marking their 31st league championship. Tevez's influence was undeniable, as his experience and skill played a pivotal role in guiding the team to domestic glory. In addition to their league success, Boca triumphed in the Copa Argentina, securing a 2-0 victory over Rosario Central in the final. *El Vasco's* double achievement of winning both the league and the national cup solidified Boca's status once again as the premier team in Argentina.

AFA have forever been changing the structure of their domestic league since it began. Unfamiliar with the phrase "if it is not broken, then don't fix it", they introduced yet another new format, dividing 30 teams into two zones, with each team playing a single round and two interzonal "classic" matches. The winners of each zone would then face off in a final to determine the champion.

Boca's performance in this format was inconsistent. They secured victories against teams like Newell's and Atlético Rafaela but suffered defeats to clubs such as Lanús and Estudiantes. The team also faced challenges in the Superclásicos against River Plate, with both encounters ending in goalless draws, yet both fixtures saw the referee brandish his yellow and red cards several times. Ultimately, Boca finished far from the top of their zone, with a record of five wins, five draws, and six losses, scoring 15 goals and conceding 13. Midway through the season, managerial changes occurred. Rodolfo Arruabarrena was dismissed due to inconsistent domestic results, and club legend Guillermo Barros Schelotto, was appointed as the new head coach.

In the Copa Libertadores, Boca showed promise by advancing to the semi finals. After a strong group stage performance, they eliminated Cerro Porteño of Paraguay in the Round of 16 and Nacional of Uruguay in the quarter finals. However, their journey ended in the semifinals against Ecuadorian side Independiente del Valle, losing the tie 3-5 on aggregate.

The Primera División underwent yet another structural change for the following domestic campaign, featuring 30 teams competing in a single round-robin format, with an additional fixture dedicated to traditional rivalries. Boca's season was highlighted by several pivotal victories. A notable triumph was the 4–2 away win against River, underscoring the team's attacking flair. Additionally, commanding performances, such as the 4–0 victory over Aldosivi and a 3–0 win against Independiente, reinforced Boca's dominance in the league.

Despite the overall success, Boca faced challenges, including a home defeat to River Plate and unexpected draws against teams like Patronato and Atlético de Rafaela. However, the squad's staying power ensured these setbacks did not derail their title aspirations.

By December, Shanghai Shenua acquired the transfer of Carlos Tevez on a contract apparently worth a staggering US$82 million over two years. Tevez's exit left a notable void in the attacking line-up, prompting the club to seek reinforcements. In response, the club secured the services of Oscar Benítez on an 18-month loan from Benfica as well as goalkeeper Agustín Rossi from Estudiantes.

The league resumed in March 2017 after a three month hiatus. Boca returned to action with a 2–0 victory over Banfield. However, the team faced a setback with a narrow defeat to Talleres at La Bombonera. Boca won five of the first nine games after the break, by May they suffered a 1-3 home defeat to River. But the Xeneize went the rest of the season unbeaten. The consistent form led them to clinch the Primera División title before the final matchday. A 2–2 draw against Olimpo secured the championship, reflecting the team's determination. The season concluded with a 2–1 victory over Unión, allowing Boca to finish the campaign on a high note, with the jubilation spilling once again onto the narrow streets of the *barrío* for hours.

For the following campaign, the Primera División underwent significant changes, being rebranded as the Superliga. Boca needed to strengthen the side for the season. Nahitan Nández, a dynamic midfielder from Peñarol, provided versatility and tenacity in the midfield. Edwin Cardona arrived on loan from Monterrey, offering creativity and technical skills essential for orchestrating offensive plays. Cristian Espinoza, the former Huracán player, arrived on loan from Villarreal. Boca started well, losing only two of their first twelve matches—winning the other ten. One of these victories included a 2-1 victory in the Superclásico at the Monumental, a game which saw nine yellow cards and two red cards brandished by experienced referee Néstor Pitana.

Staying true to his word that he would play his last professional game in the *azul y oro*, Carlos Tevez returned back to Boca for the final time after Christmas 2017. He returned back to *barrío* in different nick, seemingly treating his twenty-game tenure in China as a "holiday", to use his own word. His first goal in his third act as a Boca player, came in a 1-1 away draw with San Lorenzo.

By March, Boca faced River in the Supercopa, a highly anticipated match held at Estadio Malvinas Argentinas in Mendoza, over 1000 km from the capital. Despite dominating possession with 66%, Boca failed to convert any opportunities into goals. River capitalized on their chances, resulting in a devastating 2–0 defeat for the Xeneize.

Boca secured their 33rd Argentine Primera División title on May 9, 2018, after a hard-fought 2–2 draw against Gimnasia at the Estadio Juan Carmelo Zerillo. The match was intense from the start, with by a goal from Pablo Pérez, which was followed up with an equaliser through former Boca player Nicolás Colazo. The Xeneize responded in the second half with a goal from Ramón *"Wanchope"* Ábila. The home side equalised thanks to Brahian Alemán's strike, putting pressure on Boca. The club held on and claimed the championship with one match remaining in the season. The draw was enough to maintain their lead at the top of the table, marking their second consecutive league title under Guillermo Barros Schelotto.

Boca embarked on their 2018 Copa Libertadores campaign with high aspirations, aiming to secure their seventh title in the prestigious tournament. Placed in Group H alongside Palmeiras, Alianza Lima, and Colombian side Junior, Boca faced a challenging path from the outset.

The group stage began with a goalless draw against Alianza Lima in Peru. Subsequent matches saw Boca securing a narrow 1–0 victory over Junior at La Bombonera, followed by a 1–1 draw against Palmeiras in São Paulo. However, a 2–0 home defeat to Palmeiras raised concerns about their form. Despite these challenges, Boca managed to advance to the knockout stages, finishing second in their group.

In the Round of 16, Boca faced Paraguayan side Libertad. Demonstrating their pedigree, the team secured a 2–0 victory at home and followed it up with a 4–2 win in Paraguay, advancing with a 6–2 aggregate score. The quarter-finals pitted them against Brazilian giants Cruzeiro. A 2–0 home win, highlighted by goals from Mauro Zárate and midfielder Pablo Pérez, set the tone. A well executed defensive display in the return leg ensured a 1–1 draw, propelling Boca into the semi-finals.

The semi-final clash was against yet another Brazilian side in Palmeiras. A commanding 2–0 home win, courtesy of a brace from Darío Benedetto, provided a cushion. Despite a 2–2 draw in Brazil, Boca's aggregate superiority secured their place in the final. Awaiting them was their fiercest rival, River Plate, setting the stage for an unprecedented Superclásico in the Copa Libertadores final.

The final marked the first time in history that Boca and River contested the continent's ultimate prize. Dubbed by the press as the "final to end all finals," or the "Superfinal," this matchup was more than just a game; it was a cultural and sporting phenomenon that captivated not only Argentina but the entire footballing world.

CHAPTER EIGHTEEN

The first leg of the 2018 Copa Libertadores finals, held at La Bombonera, was initially scheduled for November 10th. However, torrential rains made the pitch unplayable. CONMEBOL considered delaying kick off by anything from two to four hours. Home fans had already started to fill La Bombonera, despite the heavily waterlogged pitch and water pouring through the stadium concourses. Eventually it was called off for 24 hours. When play finally commenced, fans were treated to a thrilling encounter. The match ended in a 2–2 draw, with Boca's *Wanchope* Ábila and Darío Benedetto finding the net, while River responded through Lucas Pratto and an own goal by Carlos Izquierdoz. This result left the tie delicately poised, with all to play for in the second leg.

The return leg was slated for November 24th at River Plate's Monumental. Anticipation was at a fever pitch, with both sets of fans eager to witness what would obviously be history. Days before, Boca had an open training session at La Bombonera, filling it to the brim and having to turn thousands more away, who filled the streets of the *barrío*, looking to gain access to see their team in simply a training session. For those who got inside, the atmosphere was insane.

On matchday, the Monumental was full long before kick-off. As the Boca's team bus approached the stadium, it was ambushed by a section of River supporters. Missiles, including bottles and stones, were hurled, shattering windows and causing injuries to several Boca players. The situation escalated when tear gas, deployed by police to disperse the crowd, inadvertently seeped into the bus, exacerbating the players' distress. The driver of the bus had passed out as a result. A board member had to take the steering wheel and get the bus out of the danger zone in Nuñez. Several Boca players and staff were deeply unwell from the tear gas, and captain Pablo Pérez, with shards of glass in his eyes, was taken to hospital.

The traumatic experience left the Boca squad in no condition to compete. The full house of River fans inside the Monumental got whispers via social media of what had been happening. Then the PA system announced a postponement of kick-off by a few hours and eventually its suspension for the day. The shameful scenes made global news. FIFA President Gianni Infantino had flown to Buenos Aires especially for the event. Allegedly he threatened Boca with disqualification if they didn't play, not taking into account what had happened, or perhaps he wasn't bothered undertaking another long flight. Infantino eventually left the stadium, surrounded by a large security presence, to a feisty reception from fans.

The game was set to be played the following day. But just a couple of hours before kick-off, with thousands of River fans inside the stadium, the fixture was called off once more. Boca had sent a press release stating that because of what happened, they wanted the second leg played in equal conditions. CONMEBOL president Alejandro Domínguez announced that the fixture would be played outside Argentina, due to safety concerns. The biggest fixture in Argentinian football was officially too big for Argentina. River were then fined for what happened outside the Monumental, and Boca sought further postponements, going so far as threatening legal action if the trophy was awarded to *los millonarios* by default. Everything made global news and the reputations of club presidents, federation presidents, everyone, it was all on the line.

There were some whispers for the final's venue. Paraguay's capital Asunción was mentioned initially, as was Miami, Doha and Medellín. The press in England had asked why the FA hadn't offered the enormous Wembley Stadium for such a prestigious event, forgetting that tens of thousands of Boca and River fans from Argentina, coupled with the sporting and political rivalry with England, a country with its own prominent football hooliganism, may not be the brightest idea. By November 29th, CONMEBOL stated that the game would be held 10,000 km away, on the other side of the Atlantic, in Real Madrid's Santiago Bernabéu Stadium.

The South American governing body stated that Madrid was chosen for various reasons, such as the stadium size and infrastructure, the neutrality of the venue and country as well as the security guarantees by the city of Madrid. Laughably they forgot the expense that many football fans would have to endure to get from Buenos Aires to the Spanish capital. Many simply couldn't afford it. But it mattered not to CONMEBOL, as tickets could easily be snapped up or sold on to many of the Argentine expats that resided in Spain. Real Madrid had also offered their historical stadium's usage for free, which may have played a big part in the decision to begin with.

This decision marked the first time a Copa Libertadores final match was held outside of South America, and the irony of hosting a cup named after the historical figures that liberated the continent from the Spanish Empire centuries before led to the phrase *Copa Conquistadores* all over social media. Many felt moving the final to Europe was a ridiculous move from CONMEBOL. Carlos Tevez was among many of the prominent figures who were strongly against the idea, and all of their protestations fell on deaf ears.

The buildup to the match in Madrid was surreal. Fans descended upon the Spanish capital, turning it into a cauldron of South American passion, including European residents, taking advantage of using the tickets that fans back in Buenos Aires were unable to use, despite the obscene pricing of hotels around Madrid that night. On December 9th, the match commenced under heightened security, with a global audience tuning in. Boca struck first, with Darío Benedetto scoring just before halftime, giving them a 1–0 lead. However, River Plate responded in the second half, with Lucas Pratto equalizing. The match proceeded to extra time, where goals from Juan Fernando Quintero and Gonzalo Martínez sealed a 3–1 victory for River Plate. This result handed River a 5–3 aggregate win, securing their fourth Copa Libertadores title. Heartbreak. The final is remembered not just for the football but, sadly, for mostly the shameful events surrounding it.

Dissatisfied with the outcome and the circumstances leading up to the relocated final, Boca filed an appeal with the Court of Arbitration for Sport (CAS). They sought River's disqualification from the 2018 Copa Libertadores, arguing that River should be held responsible for their supporters' serious misconduct, which they believed warranted severe disciplinary action. Boca had previously been suspended from the competition for the pepper spray incident at La Bombonera in 2015, so they felt that fair is fair.

After reviewing the case, CAS acknowledged that River had violated CONMEBOL's disciplinary regulations due to the extremely dangerous misconduct of their supporters. However, they deemed that stripping River from the Copa Libertadores victory would be an excessive sanction under the circumstances. Instead, they imposed a penalty requiring River to play their next two home matches in the Copa Libertadores behind closed doors to the relief of the *los millonarios* board. For Boca, the decision frustratingly marked the end of their legal avenues to contest the 2018 final's outcome.

Following what happened in Madrid, Schelotto departed from his role at La Bombonera for the MLS. In January 2019, Gustavo Alfaro was appointed as the new manager, bringing a fresh perspective to the team's strategy and performance. He was a well-seasoned manager, who had significant success at Arsenal de Sarandí. Boca entered the following domestic campaign with aspirations of securing their third consecutive league title. They brought in talent such as Ivan Marcone, Jorman Campuzano and Kevin Mac Allister, son of Carlos, who played for Boca in the early 1990s.

By May, Alfaro secured his first piece of silverware as manager of the club in the Supercopa Argentina. This annual fixture pits the winners of the Primera División against the Copa Argentina champions. On May 2, 2019, Boca faced Rosario Central at the Estadio Malvinas Argentinas in Mendoza. The match was a tense affair, with both sides unable to break the deadlock, resulting in a 0–0 draw after 90 minutes. The contest proceeded to a penalty shootout, where Boca's players held their nerve, emerging victorious with a 6–5 scoreline.

A MONTH LATER, THE Copa de la Superliga presented the club with an opportunity to secure additional silverware. The tournament, introduced to add competitive fixtures post the regular season, featured all Superliga teams in a knockout format. Boca went all the way to the final, but lost against Tigre in Córdoba.

The club managed to make world headlines with a transfer once more: Daniele De Rossi, renowned for his illustrious 18-year tenure at boyhood club Roma, put pen to paper and signed for Boca. The Italian icon officially joined on July 26th 2019 to the sheer excitement of bosteros. He turned down far more lucrative offers just to play in La Bombonera in the *azul y oro*. His debut came a few weeks after signing in a Copa Argentina match against Almagro, where he made an immediate impact by scoring a goal in a game that went to penalties which saw three new signings failing to convert in the shootout; Jan Hurtado, Eduardo Salvio, and Alexis

Mac Allister, the son of Carlos, brother of Kevin, who would later win the World Cup with Argentina and excel in England's Premier League with Liverpool.

Alfaro's team went unbeaten right up until October. The Superclásico at the Monumental finished goalless, but stretched Boca's unbeaten run at the opponent's stadium across town into almost a decade. The Copa Libertadores semi finals pitted the two arch-enemies once more. The incidents from the final almost a year before were still fresh in memory for both sets of fans. The first leg took place at the Monumental, where River secured a 2–0 victory. Goals from Rafael Santos Borré and Ignacio Fernández provided River with a substantial advantage. The return leg occurred three weeks later at La Bombonera. Despite Boca winning 1–0, courtesy of a goal from Jan Hurtado, River advanced to the final with a 2–1 aggregate score. Both legs saw no less than 14 yellow cards and a single red card being shown. River eventually lost the final to Brazilian side Flamengo in Peru's Estadio Monumental, home of Universitario de Deportes.

Boca's final handful of games for 2019 had mixed results. Despite a 5-1 over Arsenal, they battled to find a win to close out the calendar year. Gustavo Alfaro knew his time as manager was up. He was replaced by a familiar face Miguel Ángel Russo as manager. Russo was appointed the day before New Year's Eve, marking his return to the club after previously leading the team to a Copa Libertadores title glory, just over a decade before.

Earlier in the month, Boca held a highly anticipated presidential election. More than 38,000 members participated, making it one of the most significant elections in the club's history. Jorge Amor Ameal won the election with 52.84% of the vote, alongside his running mate Juan Román Riquelme, who took charge of Boca's football department. Their victory ended the leadership of Daniel Angelici, whose preferred candidate, Christian Gribaudo, finished second with 30.60% of the vote. José Beraldi came third with 16.36%.

In January 2020, Italian midfielder Daniele De Rossi announced his retirement on January 6, citing family reasons. The World Cup winner only managed two full 90 minutes in his brief stint at La Boca. With a heavy heart, De Rossi left Buenos Aires back for his homeland, with lots of affection from *bosteros*.

The club brought in Guillermo *"Pol"* Fernández from Cruz Azul, the former youth player who left the club five years prior. Miguel Ángel Russo's first match in charge during his second tenure as Boca played to a 0–0 draw against Independiente at La Bombonera, with Riquelme looking on. The team resumed the campaign with a crucial 2–1 victory over Talleres. They followed it up with a 2–0 win against Atlético Tucumán, then delivered a commanding 4–0 triumph over Central Córdoba. Their dominance continued with a 3–0 victory over Godoy Cruz and another emphatic 4–0 win against Colón. These results set up a dramatic final round, where Boca faced Gimnasia at La Bombonera, managed by a certain Argentinian legend.

The team faced Gimnasia at La Bombonera on March 7th, in a match that would decide the Superliga Argentina title. The night was filled with tension and anticipation, not only because Boca had the chance to overtake River Plate at the top of the table, but also due to the emotional return of Diego Maradona. Managing Gimnasia, Maradona stepped onto the pitch of the stadium where he became a legend, greeted by a thunderous ovation from the Boca faithful. Despite his siding with the losing candidate in the recent presidential elections, the presence of *El Diego* was a spectacle in itself, as La Bombonera erupted in chants of his name, a reminder of his unbreakable bond with the club. Before the match, Boca's board presented him with a commemorative plaque, and Maradona, visibly moved, acknowledged the crowd.

Before kick-off, Carlos Tevez walked over to Maradona and embraced him on the lips. One Boca legend who wore number 10 to another. Once the game began, Boca, under Russo's guidance, tried intensely to break down Gimnasia's defence. The nerves in the stadium were palpable, with every missed chance heightening the tension. The breakthrough finally came in the 72nd minute when Tevez, embodying the spirit of Boca, rifled a shot past the goalkeeper after a layoff from Ramón Ábila. The stadium exploded in celebration, knowing that with River Plate failing to win their match against Atlético Tucumán, Boca was moments away from the title.

As the final whistle blew, Boca Juniors were crowned champions, overtaking River in the last round of the season. The triumph was sealed in front of Maradona, whose return to La Bombonera had added an emotional weight to an already historic night. He left the field with a bittersweet expression, proud of the reception he had received but defeated by the club that had defined so much of his life. For Boca, it was not just another title—it was a moment of redemption, passion, and history colliding under the lights of La Bombonera. The *barrío* once again was lit up by fireworks.

AFA had decided to send the trophy to La Bombonera, on the chance that Boca might win the title against Gimnasia. Instead, they would receive the silverware in the first Copa Superliga fixture, scheduled for later in the month. However, football was suspended and later canceled due to the COVID-19 pandemic, which spread around the entire globe, shutting down almost all industries in every country.

The club officially ended their long-standing partnership with Nike and transitioned to Adidas as their new kit supplier. This marked a significant change, as Nike had been Boca sponsor and clothing manufacturer since 1996. Some of the most iconic Boca shirts were designed and made by the American company. But Adidas is almost always more popular among fans. The iconic three stripes, like the one Maradona wore in 1981, was making its return. The switch to Adidas was the result of a new ten-year contract, making it one of the most lucrative sponsorship deals in Argentine football history.

Boca played the first two Copa Libertadores games in March. The pandemic had other ideas, and the competition resumed in September. Boca returned to action with a strong performance, securing a 2–0 away win against Libertad. They continued their winning form with a 1–0 victory over Independiente Medellín in Colombia. A goalless draw with Libertad at home followed, but they closed out the group stage with a convincing 3–0 win over Caracas. With these results, Boca finished at the top of their group and advanced to the knockout rounds.

But soon after, shockwaves were sent around the world, as millions mourned the loss of a player who had transcended the sport. Diego Maradona, died in Buenos Aires on November 25th 2020. He had been struggling with health issues for years, exacerbated by his well-documented battles with addiction and lifestyle choices. In early November 2020, he underwent emergency brain surgery for a subdural hematoma, a condition caused by head trauma. He was released from the hospital on November 11 to recover at his home but his condition remained fragile.

On the morning of November 25, Maradona suffered a heart attack at his residence in Dique Luján, just north of Buenos Aires.

Despite efforts to revive him, he was pronounced dead at the scene. He was 60-years old. The news was confirmed by his lawyer and close friend Matías Morla, and within minutes, tributes poured in from around the globe. Argentina immediately declared three days of national mourning, with President Alberto Fernández, himself a supporter of Diego's first club Argentinos Juniors, calling the former player "the greatest of all time" and ordering his body to lie in state at the Casa Rosada, the presidential palace that lies on the east side of the Plaza de Mayo. Thousands of fans gathered outside, chanting his name and paying their final respects. Images flooded social media of the incredibly rare sight of Boca and River fans decked out in their club colours, holding each other, crying over the icon who had brought them together.

The days following Maradona's death were filled with emotional scenes as Argentina and the football world grieved. His coffin was on public display at the Casa Rosada, and over one million people came to bid farewell, many draped in Argentina or Boca flags. The overwhelming crowd led to chaotic scenes, with clashes between police and fans as authorities struggled to manage the massive turnout. The government was forced to cut the wake short, and Maradona's body was transported to Jardín Bella Vista cemetery, where he was buried in a private ceremony alongside his parents.

Around the world, football paid tribute to the legend who had defined generations. Stadiums dimmed their lights, teams observed moments of silence, and players dedicated goals in his memory. Napoli, where Maradona reached legendary status in the late 1980s, officially renamed their stadium the *Stadio Diego Armando Maradona* in his honour.

Maradona's death left a void in football that will never be filled. His name, his moments of brilliance, and his spirit will live on in the memories of those who watched him play. From the streets of Buenos Aires, from the temple of La Bombonera, from the Camp Nou, from the packed stadium of Naples, from the World Cup to the local playgrounds where kids still dream of being the next Diego, his legacy is eternal. He was more than just a footballer—he was an icon, a flawed genius, a symbol of joy, defiance, and greatness.

Four days later, Boca played against Newell's at La Bombonera. The game carried immense emotional weight as in attendance was Maradona's daughter, Dalma, who watched the match from her father's private box, as one of the very few in attendance that night due to measures put in place because of the pandemic. An Edwin Cardona brace sealed a victory on the night, but it was after the first goal, the Colombian and his team-mates, wearing Maradona jerseys, ran over to the side of the pitch and looked up to the stands, where Maradona's daughter Dalma was seated, and gave her an ovation. An act that reduced her to tears.

In January 2021, Boca faced Santos in the Copa Libertadores semi-finals, a highly anticipated clash between two of South America's most storied clubs. The first leg was played on January 6 at La Bombonera, where Boca struggled to get past Santos' defence. Despite a few half-chances, the game ended in a 0–0 draw, leaving everything to be decided in the return leg in Brazil.

The second leg took place on January 13 at Vila Belmiro, where Boca suffered a 3–0 defeat, ending their hopes of reaching the final. Santos took control early, with Diego Pituca scoring in the 16th minute to give the Brazilian side the lead. Boca's situation worsened in the second half when Yeferson Soteldo doubled Santos' advantage in the 49th minute with a stunning goal. Just three minutes later, Lucas Braga sealed the result, making it 3–0. Boca's frustrations boiled over, and Frank Fabra was sent off in the 56th minute, leaving the team with ten men. With this result, Boca were eliminated, and Santos advanced to the Copa Libertadores final against Palmeiras. The defeat was a bitter disappointment for the Xeneize, who had hoped to win their first Libertadores title since 2007.

The club participated in a tournament organized amid the ongoing COVID-19 pandemic, which continued to affect football activities worldwide. The competition featured 26 teams divided into two zones, with matches played without spectators to comply with health protocols.

Boca's campaign began on February 14, 2021, with a 2–2 draw against Gimnasia at La Bombonera. Throughout the group stage, they experienced a mix of results, including a notable 7–1 away victory over Vélez Sarsfield on March 7th. They also faced setbacks, such as a 2–1 home defeat to Talleres de Córdoba on March 21, 2021. Despite these fluctuations, Boca secured enough points to advance to the knockout stages.

In the quarterfinals on May 16th, Boca faced their arch-rivals, River, at La Bombonera. The match ended in a 1–1 draw, leading to a penalty shootout, which Boca won 4–2, propelling them to the semifinals. However, on May 31th, in the semi-finals held at Estadio Bicentenario in San Juan, Boca played Racing. After a goalless draw, the match proceeded to penalties, where Boca was eliminated 4–2, ending their pursuit of the title.

Another icon of the club, Carlos Tevez announced his retirement from professional football on June 4th, 2021, bringing an end to a remarkable career that spanned over two decades. His decision came nearly a year after leaving Boca, the club where he had started and ended his playing days. In an emotional interview, Tevez revealed that his father's passing four months prior had deeply affected him, and he no longer felt the motivation to continue playing. He admitted that despite receiving offers from various clubs, his heart was simply no longer in the game.

His final stint at the club was marked by a league title win in 2020, where he played a crucial role in securing the championship. However, the emotional burden of personal loss, combined with the physical demands of football, led him to step back. Tevez's name is forever etched in stone as a legend of Boca for *bosteros*.

In the 2021 season, Boca faced numerous challenges and transitions. The year commenced with the departure of key players,To bolster the squad, Boca secured the signings of Nicolás Orsini from Lanús, and Norberto Briasco and Esteban Rolón from Huracán, aiming to inject fresh talent into the team.

The team's performance in the domestic league was inconsistent. Under the management of Miguel Ángel Russo, Boca struggled to find form, leading to his dismissal in August. Sebastián Battaglia, the former player beloved in La Boca, was appointed as the new manager, under whom the team showed improvement. Boca concluded the Primera División in fourth place, a position that fell short of the club's high expectations.

Despite the league challenges, Boca excelled in the Copa Argentina, going all the way to the final, where they faced Talleres de Córdoba at the Estadio Madre de Ciudades in Santiago del Estero. The match was intensely contested, with both teams striving for dominance but unable to break the deadlock, resulting in a 0–0 draw after regular time. The pivotal moment occurred in the 65th minute when Boca's Juan Ramírez received a red card, reducing his team to ten men and adding pressure to their defensive efforts.

The championship was ultimately decided by a penalty shootout. Boca displayed composure and precision, converting all five of their penalties. In contrast, Talleres faltered when Héctor Fertoli's attempt was saved by Boca's goalkeeper, Agustín Rossi. This crucial save secured a 5–4 victory in the shootout for the Xeneize, earning them their fourth Copa Argentina title. This triumph granted them qualification for the group stage of the 2022 Copa Libertadores.

The following year, Boca embarked on a campaign marked by strategic player movements and managerial decisions. The return of Darío Benedetto was a significant highlight in the transfer market, bolstering the team's attacking options. Additionally, the squad was strengthened by the acquisitions of Guillermo 'Pol' Fernández, who rejoined the club, Nicolás Figal, and goalkeeper Leandro Brey. Conversely, the team saw the departures of players such as Ramón Ábila, Edwin Cardona, Walter Bou, Agustín Obando, Lisandro López, and several youth players who went out on loan.

The tournament structure featured 28 teams divided into two zones of 14 clubs each. Boca commenced their journey with a 1–1 draw against Colón at La Bombonera. They secured their first victory by defeating Aldosivi 2–1 in Mar del Plata. Throughout the group stage, Boca's performance was a mix of wins, draws, and a notable home defeat to Huracán, where they lost 1–0. Despite these fluctuations, Boca accumulated sufficient points to advance to the knockout stages.

The semifinal pitted Boca against Racing Club in a tense encounter. The match concluded in a 0–0 draw, leading to a penalty shootout. Boca's players exhibited composure under pressure, emerging victorious with a 6–5 scoreline in the shootout, thereby earning their spot in the final.

On May 22, 2022, Boca clinched the Copa de la Liga Profesional title with a commanding 3–0 victory over Tigre at the Estadio Mario Alberto Kempes in Córdoba. The match saw Boca take the lead just before halftime when Marcos Rojo scored with a header. In the second half, Frank Fabra doubled the advantage with a remarkable long-range goal, and Luis Vázquez sealed the win with another header in the closing minutes.

The victory also secured them a spot in the 2023 Copa Libertadores and the 2022 Trofeo de Campeones. The team's performance in the final showcased their tactical prowess and clinical finishing, reflecting a well-executed game plan by manager Sebastián Battaglia. Throughout the tournament, several players made significant contributions. Darío Benedetto emerged as the team's top scorer, netting seven goals. Winger Sebastián Villa also played a pivotal role, featuring in all 17 matches and scoring five goals. Defensively, Marcos Rojo was instrumental, not only in defence but also contributing two goals.

Having gone through the group stage, Sebastián Battaglia was dismissed as Boca Juniors' manager on July 6th, following the team's elimination from the Copa Libertadores Round of 16 against Corinthians. The decision came after a goalless draw at La Bombonera, where Boca was knocked out on penalties. Despite leading Boca to two domestic titles—the 2021 Copa Argentina and the 2022 Copa de la Liga Profesional—Battaglia faced increasing pressure due to inconsistent performances and internal tensions within the club. His departure marked the end of his first senior managerial role, having initially taken charge as an interim coach in 2021 before being appointed permanently. Hugo Ibarra was named as his replacement on an interim basis, as Boca sought stability for the remainder of the season.

Boca's league campaign started inconsistently, with early defeats to Unión, Banfield, and Argentinos Juniors, raising doubts about their ability to contend for the championship. However, under Ibarra's leadership, the team steadily improved, adopting a more pragmatic approach. The defence, led by Marcos Rojo, Carlos Zambrano, and goalkeeper Rossi, became more solid, while the attacking trio of Darío Benedetto, Sebastián Villa, and Luca Langoni provided crucial goals at key moments. Boca's midfield, featuring Alan Varela, *Pol* Fernández, and Juan Ramírez, was instrumental in controlling the tempo of games. Their improved form was reflected in an impressive winning streak, which propelled them to the top of the table.

One of the defining moments of Boca's season came in the Superclásico against River at La Bombonera. In a high-stakes encounter, Boca secured a 1–0 victory, with Darío Benedetto scoring the decisive goal. The win was not only significant in terms of league standings but also served as a morale booster, strengthening the belief that Boca could go all the way. From that point, the team continued to grind out results, securing narrow but vital wins against Lanús, Vélez Sarsfield, and Gimnasia, as they edged closer to the title.

The championship race reached its climax on October 23rd 2022, in a dramatic final round. Boca needed a victory against Independiente at La Bombonera to secure the title, but the match ended in a tense 2–2 draw. However, their closest challenger, Racing, had the chance to snatch the title but suffered a 2–1 defeat to River, ensuring Boca finished at the top with 52 points. The chaotic and emotional final day perfectly encapsulated Boca's season—full of ups and downs, drama, and a fighting spirit that ultimately led them to their 35th title.

By the following month, the World Cup was being held in Qatar, despite the numerous protests about human rights abuses, particularly concerning the treatment of migrant workers involved in constructing stadiums and infrastructure. Investigations by organizations such as Amnesty International and Human Rights Watch revealed that thousands of workers from countries like Nepal, India, and Bangladesh faced exploitative labor conditions, including unpaid wages, excessive working hours, and unsafe environments. Qatar's kafala system, which tied workers to their employers and restricted their ability to change jobs or leave the country, was widely criticized as a form of modern slavery. Reports estimated that thousands of migrant workers died due to extreme heat and poor working conditions, though the exact numbers remain disputed. Beyond labor rights, concerns were also raised about freedom of speech, LGBTQ+ rights, and the repression of activists, as the Qatari government imposed strict laws that limited personal freedoms. Despite international pressure, significant reforms were slow and often ineffective, overshadowing the tournament with ethical and humanitarian concerns.

The concerns fell on deaf ears, and the World Cup went ahead. Money talks. The pundits who spoke about concern in the months and years prior to the tournament, still went to the tournament to cover it. While former Manchester United and Ireland captain, Roy Keane, was one of the few who said on-air that the tournament should not have been held in Qatar, it ultimately made no odds as he said it from the television studio within the stadium in Doha.

For Argentina, they needed to end their World Cup drought. It was likely the last chance saloon for 35-year-old Lionel Messi, who for some, despite his consistent world-class play for almost two decades, needed to lift the famous trophy in order to be on par with Maradona. Only one player from Argentina's domestic league made the squad headed for Qatar, River's goalkeeper Franco Armani. The majority of the squad were based in Europe, primarily Spain, Italy and England.

Argentina's tournament began with a shocking 2–1 defeat to Saudi Arabia, one of the biggest upsets in World Cup history. However, the loss served as a wake-up call, and Lionel Scaloni's team responded with back-to-back 2–0 victories over Mexico and Poland, securing qualification for the knockout stages. In the Round of 16, Argentina defeated Australia 2–1, with Lionel Messi scoring a brilliant goal in what was his 1,000th career match. The quarter-final against the Netherlands turned into an intense battle, as Argentina squandered a 2–0 lead, conceding twice in the final moments. The match went to penalties, where Emiliano *"Dibu"* Martínez emerged as the hero, saving two spot-kicks to send Argentina to the semifinals.

The final against France was an all-time classic, with Argentina leading 2–0 before Kylian Mbappé scored twice in quick succession to force extra time. Messi put Argentina ahead again, but Mbappé completed his hat-trick with a late penalty, sending the game to a shootout. Once again, *Dibu* Martínez made a crucial save, and Gonzalo Montiel converted the winning penalty to give Argentina their third World Cup title, ending a 36-year wait. Messi, crowned Player of the Tournament, finally lifted the trophy that had eluded him for so long, cementing his legacy as one of football's greatest icons forever.

Argentinian football wasn't finished in the Middle East. Boca faced Racing Club in the inaugural Supercopa Internacional at the Hazza bin Zayed Stadium in Al Ain, United Arab Emirates. This newly established competition, organized by AFA in collaboration with the Abu Dhabi Sports Council, was designed to pit the reigning champions of Argentina's Primera División against the winners of the Trofeo de Campeones. The match concluded with a 2–1 victory for Racing Club, who secured the title by overturning an early deficit.

The team started the year under Hugo Ibarra, who had been in charge since mid-2022. Boca's campaign began with high expectations after winning the 2022 league title, but early performances raised concerns about the team's ability to defend its crown. By March, poor results and a lack of convincing performances led to Ibarra's dismissal. Mariano Herrón briefly took over as interim manager before Jorge Almirón was appointed in April to guide the team for the rest of the season.

Boca's Primera División campaign was inconsistent. They started with a 1–0 victory over Tucumán, but early defeats against Talleres de Córdoba and Banfield signaled trouble. A rough patch in April saw the team lose three consecutive matches against Colón, San Lorenzo, and Estudiantes, putting their title hopes in jeopardy. Despite the setbacks, Boca secured key wins over Racing Club (3–1) and Belgrano (2–0) to regain momentum. However, the inconsistency continued, and the team struggled to challenge for the title. By the end of the season, Boca finished in 7th place, far from the championship fight, marking a disappointing league campaign.

The club completed the high-profile signing of Edinson Cavani in July 2023, bringing the Uruguayan striker to Argentina after years of speculation about a potential move. Cavani, one of the greatest Uruguayan forwards of his generation, joined Boca on a free transfer after parting ways with Valencia, where he had spent a single season in La Liga. His arrival was seen as a major coup for

Boca, as he had previously played for Napoli, Paris Saint-Germain, and Manchester United, winning league titles and domestic cups in Europe while scoring over 400 career goals. The club had pursued Cavani for years, and the transfer was finally made possible after he terminated his contract with Valencia, expressing his lifelong dream of playing for Boca and experiencing the passion of La Bombonera. Boca presented him in front of thousands of fans, welcoming him as the marquee signing for their Copa Libertadores campaign, with hopes that his experience and goal-scoring ability would lead the club to continental glory.

Cavani made his debut in August and quickly became a focal point of Boca's attack, though he battled with injuries and adapting to Argentine football at first. Despite not producing his best form immediately, his leadership and presence added immense value to the squad, particularly as Boca pushed for the Libertadores title, reaching the final against Fluminense. His signing represented not only a boost in quality on the field but also a statement of Boca's ambition to remain a powerhouse in South American football, showing they could still attract world-class talent.

Following a poor domestic campaign, the Copa Libertadores proved to be Boca's saving grace, as the club embarked on a deep run in the tournament. The club had an impressive campaign, making it all the way to the final, which was held at the famous Maracanã Stadium in Rio de Janeiro, where Boca faced Fluminense in a highly anticipated showdown. Boca, seeking their seventh Libertadores title, put up an enormous fight against the Brazilian side, relying on their strong defensive structure and the goalkeeping heroics of Sergio Romero, who had been a key figure throughout the tournament. Fluminense took the lead in the first half with a goal from Germán Cano, but Boca responded in the second half when the brilliant and criminally under-rated Luis Advíncula scored a stunning long-range effort to level the match at 1–1, sending it into extra time. However, Fluminense regained control in the added period, and substitute, the exquisitely named forward John Kennedy netted the decisive goal, sealing a 2–1 victory for the Brazilian club. The match ended in controversy, with Kennedy receiving a second yellow card for his goal celebration, leaving Fluminense to finish the game with ten men. Despite a late push from Boca, they were unable to find an equalizer, and Fluminense lifted their first-ever Copa Libertadores trophy, while Boca was left heartbroken after coming so close once again to continental glory.

In tandem with the continental tournament, was the Copa de la Liga Profesional, Boca faced a challenging campaign, failing to advance beyond the group stage. The tournament, structured into two zones of 14 teams each, required clubs to finish in the top positions to progress to the knockout rounds. Boca's performance was inconsistent, culminating in a record of 5 wins, 3 draws, and 6 losses over 14 matches. Despite notable signings, including Marcelo Saracchi, Lucas Blondel, Lucas Janson, and Ezequiel Bullaude, the team struggled to find form. Their campaign began positively with a 3–1 victory over Platense, but subsequent defeats to teams like Sarmiento, Tigre, and Defensa y Justicia hindered their momentum. A significant setback occurred with a 0–2 home loss to arch-rivals River on October 1. Although the Xeneize secured wins against Unión and Newell's later in the tournament, these results were insufficient to secure a spot in the knockout phase, marking a disappointing exit for the club.

In the 2024 season, Boca experienced a series of challenges and transitions across various competitions. The year commenced with the Copa de la Liga Profesional, where Boca aimed to improve upon their previous performances. However, the team were battling to find consistency, leading to an early exit from the tournament. This setback prompted internal evaluations and increased pressure on the coaching staff to deliver better results in the upcoming competitions.

The Copa Argentina presented an opportunity for redemption. Boca began their campaign with a solid 3–0 victory over Central Norte de Salta. They continued their progress by defeating Almirante Brown 2–1 in the Round of 32. In the Round of 16, Boca faced Talleres, and after a 1–1 draw, they advanced by winning 8–7 in a dramatic penalty shootout. The quarter-final against Gimnasia was particularly eventful; the match ended 1–1, and Boca triumphed 2–1 in the penalty shootout. This game was sadly marred by fan violence, requiring intervention from club president Juan Román Riquelme, who personally addressed the supporters to calm the situation. In the semi-finals, Boca's journey ended with a 4–3 loss to Vélez, concluding their Copa Argentina aspirations.

In the Primera División, Boca's performance was marked by inconsistency. The season began with a 1–0 loss to Atlético Tucumán, followed by a 4–2 victory over Central Córdoba. Throughout the campaign, Boca struggled to maintain momentum, experiencing a mix of wins, draws, and losses. Notably, they suffered a 1–0 home defeat to arch-rivals River on September 21. A series of poor results, including three consecutive losses, led to the resignation of head coach Diego Martínez on September 29. Former player Fernando Gago was appointed as the new manager but faced challenges in stabilizing the team's form. Despite these hurdles, Boca managed a late-season resurgence, securing crucial victories that enabled them to qualify for the preliminary phase of the Copa Libertadores, finishing the league in a respectable position.

The 2024 season highlighted both the strengths and the areas needing improvement for Boca. While the team faced early exits and managerial changes, their ability to rally in the latter part of the season demonstrated potential. The intervention by Riquelme during the Copa Argentina quarter-final underscored the club's commitment to maintaining order and focus amidst challenges. As Boca prepares for the next season, the experiences of 2024 serve as lessons to build upon, aiming for greater consistency and success in domestic and international arenas.

But results will always fluctuate. For Boca fans, it really is more than just supporting a football club; it is a way of life, a deep-rooted passion that transcends generations. From the moment a person is born into a Boca-supporting family, they are introduced to a culture of unwavering loyalty, emotion, and devotion. Boca is not just a team; it represents the working-class struggle, the determination of the people, and the pride of La Bombonera, one of the most electrifying stadiums in the world. Fans don't just watch matches; they live them, pouring their hearts out with chants, flags, and an unmatched atmosphere that intimidates opponents and inspires the players. Boca have fans all around the world, who are mesmerised by how the club runs and the culture which it generates. Supporting Boca means embracing an identity, one filled with highs, lows, and unforgettable moments.

The emotional rollercoaster of following Boca is unlike any other. There are moments of ecstatic joy, like winning league titles, conquering South America with Copa Libertadores triumphs, and legendary victories over arch-rivals River. But just as important are the painful moments—the near misses, the heartbreaks, the controversial decisions, and the bitter defeats. Through it all, Boca fans remain steadfast. Of course losses hurt, but they never break the spirit of *bosteros*. They take pride in suffering for their team because, for Boca fans, passion is unconditional. Every matchday, they pack La Bombonera, knowing that their voices and presence can change the course of a game.

A Boca fan carries the club in their daily life. It is not just about football; it is about tradition, family, and pride. The blue and gold colors are sacred, worn with honour on the streets of Buenos Aires and across the world. The club's history is passed down like folklore—stories of Diego Maradona's magic, Juan Román Riquelme's brilliance, Hugo Gatti's heroics, Silvio Marzolini's greatness, Roberto Mouzo's consistency, Roberto Cherro's and Martín Palermo's goal scoring dominance, Carlos Tevez's power, and countless legendary moments are told and retold. Whether they are at the stadium, watching from home, or following from another country, Boca fans feel an unbreakable connection to their team. The phrase *"Boca es Boca"* (Boca is Boca) is more than a slogan—it represents something unique, something that cannot be explained, only experienced.

To be a Boca fan is to be part of a global brotherhood of passion, tenacity, and unwavering loyalty. It means believing in the impossible, standing by the club no matter what, and always expecting greatness. Whether celebrating in the streets after a championship or singing in defiance after a tough loss, Boca fans know that their love for the club is eternal. The club's anthem, *"Boca, mi buen amigo"*, says it best—Boca is more than just a club; it is a lifelong companion, a love that never fades, and a legacy that continues through generations. And to think it all started with some young men at a park bench in Plaza Solís in La Boca in 1905.

AFTERWORD

My relationship with Boca Juniors started out a few decades ago. Being based in Ireland, watching live Argentinian football was near impossible up until relatively recently. I first encountered Boca whe Diego Maradona re-joined the club in 1995, which made headlines in the sports newspapers and television programmes. Synonymous with the club, Maradona was, and still is, my favourite player.

Around that time there was an early morning TV show on (I think) Channel 4 which used to show a variety of sporting events around the world. Occasionally they would show what was going on in South America, such as the Copa Libertadores. I was taken aback by it immediately; a bed of white ticker tape all over the pitch, the aggressive style of football and, most prominently, *la avalancha* when there was a goal scored; the fans behind the goals, rushing dangerously forward in unison. This exotic and insane sporting fandom was deeply exciting to me.

It wasn't until the mid 2000's when an Irish sportswear chain, Lifestyle Sports, started stocking en masse the 2005 Boca Juniors centenary jersey by Nike for a very affordable price. To this day, I have no idea why, but I'm assuming they were offered them cheap and they sold them cheap. But I was first in line to buy mine.

Around this time, YouTube became the popular way to watch videos online. So while my friends were watching English Premier League footage, I would watch incredibly low resolution videos of highlights of some Boca matches. Around this time eBay also became a common online marketplace, and I purchased literally dozens of Boca jerseys, including an original 1981 jersey which has since very regrettably been lost in one of the several house-moving operations I've undertaken over the past decade or two.

I've always been a musician. Since I was a young teenager. I played my first gig at 15, underage in a dodgy pub in Dublin's city centre. I started out as a drummer with my friends, before moving off the drum stool and being what Noel Gallagher refers to as "the jazz hands at the front", with just a microphone and a guitar. Inspired by the likes of Paul Weller, I mostly played acoustic numbers that I wrote. Despite playing legendary venues such as Dublin's Olympia Theatre, Vicar Street and touring across continental Europe and the east coast of the US, I didn't love what I was doing. There were some decent songs, but they mostly didn't move me. I seemed to be making the same type of music everyone else was making. I found it a little boring, to be honest. In early 2015, I went to a recording studio and made a 1970s-style punk song. And that changed everything.

During the golden age of Facebook, I was a regular commentator of Boca's social media networks. And my comments would regularly be picked up by fans of the club. *"Who the hell is this Irish guy? And why does he like Boca?"* I get it. It's unusual. But I love it. At the time, I was only newly married and had an infant daughter, so I hadn't recorded any music in almost five years. I had been experimenting with synthesizers and more electronic equipment for a side-project that would later be called The Swedish Railway Orchestra, but I very swiftly made a decision that I would write and record a rock song about Boca Juniors.

It was written in about 20 minutes. It only had a few chords that and a key shift that, if memory serves me correctly, were mostly inspired by "Oliver's Army" by Elvis Costello. It was recorded in January 2015 in a very impressive home recording studio of a guy named Dessie Brosnan, who I knew via Bohemian Football Club (Ireland's number one club - check them out). I played all the instruments, recorded it in an afternoon and got the final mix from Dessie some days later. These were the last days of downloading music as one of the most common ways to consume music, streaming would overtake it within a year or two. I didn't make any plans for it apart from posting it on social media, so I was hoping that maybe I would get fifty downloads, and I'll use that money for a couple of pints. There was no plan, no PR company and certainly no record label behind it. But it spread like wildfire in Argentina. My following on social media went way into the thousands overnight, verified blue ticks were popping up all over the place, requests for interviews filled my inbox. The song was downloaded thousands upon thousands of times in Argentina, thrusting it into the nation's actual charts. There wasn't even a music video for it.

I wasn't ready for all of that. But it was happening, so I went along with it. I tried to reply to every single person that contacted me. To my astonishment, Boca Juniors reached out, inviting me to visit La Bombonera. Naturally I said yes without thinking about it. It occurred to me that perhaps I could arrange some concerts while in the Argentine capital. I must have emailed every venue in the city. From massive ones to small ones. Eventually, a promoter got in touch saying he'd love to have me as the main event for a weekly concert they put on in a massive Irish pub, just off Av. 9 de Julio.

Also, a promoter from an enormous club in Palermo Hollywood, the very fancy suburb renowned for its nightlife, got in touch. They offered me a very generous amount of cash to DJ in the club for an hour. So naturally I agreed.

In May 2015, after a gruelling 15 hours in the air, I landed in Ezeiza airport, on the outskirts of Buenos Aires from Dublin, via Madrid's Barajas airport. I was aware of comments from younger Boca fans who said "we should meet Rob at the airport". I'm not joking you, they literally wanted to do that thing, like when a footballer joins a team, fans meet them at the airport and dons them in a scarf of the club, and sing the teams songs. I didn't offer my flight details, probably out of nervousness. I regret that a touch, I should have gone for it, as it would have been hilarious. I had only arrived at my hotel about twenty minutes, at the NH Collection Lancaster, on the corner of Av. Cordoba and Reconquista, when the phone rang. It was Boca's press office. "See you in an hour," they said. Not much time to take in a badly needed nap or to even get ready, so off I went.

I walked to the famous Plaza de Mayo, a few blocks south of my hotel, and jumped into a cab. The journey took me the whole way south on Av. Paseo Colón. I could see the Parque Lezama to my right, the leafy, hilly park at a busy junction before you enter La Boca. The cab kept going on Av. Almirante Brown, the street named after the founder of the Argentinian Navy, I knew this because he was from Foxford in County Mayo. The Irish have long had a history of going to Argentina. Here I was, a confused and excited Irish man on my own journey in Argentina. The car turned right onto Brandsen. I had seen that name so regularly. Brandsen 805 is the address of the stadium. The streets were becoming more pronounced with the famous yellow and gold. Then suddenly, there it was, right in front of me, La Bombonera.

I told the security at the door who I was, and after a few minutes' wait, the two staff members from the press office ushered me inside. This was what it must feel like to win the lottery. I am literally inside La Bombonera. They gave me a grand tour of the stadium, the dressing rooms, the museum, before being led onto the pitch. I was having my photograph taken when suddenly a replica of the Copa Libertadores was thrust upon me. I cradled it in my arms while posing with a stupid jet-lagged grin on my face, when all of a sudden I heard some tourists taking a tour of the stadium from the confines of the stands say something along the lines of "why is that gringo on the fucking pitch?"

I LEFT THE STADIUM rejuvenated with energy I wasn't sure I even had. That night was gig number one of two. A club in Palermo Hollywood called Jager Velvet Club. Its capacity was around

600 patrons or so. When I got to the venue, it became very apparent that this crowd was not my crowd. This is where the middle to upper class of Buenos Aires came to dance to music I could only describe as not-my-cup-of-tea. I stood on this platform/stage thing where there were some state of the art DJ decks as well as some other faux fancy items, such as a VIP couch just behind the DJ booth with a table and bottles of some designer vodka that you or I would need to remortgage our houses to afford. The beautiful and rich of the country's capital, decked out in designer clothing eyeing me up and down. *Who the fuck is this guy?*" I hadn't been briefed by the promoter of what to do or expect. Thinking that legendary rock bands like The Stone Roses, The Fall or The Strokes would go down like a lead balloon in this venue, the music surely must be of the electronic flavour. So I think I played some LCD Soundsystem remixes. Perhaps some Hot Chip. Maybe a squeeze of Basement Jaxx. That kind of thing. I don't think I set the room on fire that night, so to speak. I let the resident DJs back onto the decks and the style changed to more reggaeton beats and other such things uninteresting to me. I got paid and got out there.

The following night, the gig was at an Irish pub called Temple Bar on Marcelo Torcuato de Alvear, just off the Av. 9 de Julio, the city's main thoroughfare. It was a really big bar with a stage just at the entrance. The promoters held weekly live events at the bar, with a live radio show beside the stage, broadcasting the live events with commentary in between acts. I actually thought it was a good set up. The main promoter was a guy called Jeronimo, and his brother Joaquin was the singer in a relatively well known local band called Blazer, who had recently played a gig at Vélez Sarsfield's stadium. The entire team of the promotion company consisted of maybe a dozen or so people, mostly all in their 20's, and they were all there that night.

The first few bands were okay. Not bad, not terrible. Just okay. The venue was filling up. There was no backstage, so I ended up meeting a lot of people and posing for photographs with a lot of people. Some would complain about that, but they need to basically shut the fuck up. It was a novelty for me, so I was trying to enjoy my fifteen minutes. The promoters didn't do pre-sale tickets, so I was glad to see that before I took the stage, it had eventually sold out. I was due to do an hour long DJ set, but before I went on, there was a tribute band to local legendary band Sumo doing a 45 minute set. I had heard something about this band, but I was told by people in the months prior that Sumo are this incredible band, led by the late Luca Prodan, an interesting Italian-born wordsmith, with links to the post-punk scene in England, with bands like the phenomenal Joy Division. Sumo are a highly influential band for Spanish language rock bands, but are only really known in South America. Without question, they're a household name in Argentina. I watched this tribute band, and listened. Songs like "La Rubia Tarada" and "Mejor No Hablar De Ciertas Cosas" gripped me instantly. I think I was a new fan of this band. My own gig went well. People turned up in Boca shirts. I played songs, people enjoyed themselves, I drank multiple pints of Quilmes. I shook hands with people, took selfies, and had the craic with everyone. It all ended well. I retreated back to my hotel on foot just a few blocks away and had a celebratory pint in my hotel room and looked out at the busy Avenida Cordoba, amazed at what happened.

The next couple of days, I spent the time doing a few interviews, which went okay. Except for one incident with a young writer who interviewed me for some publication, in a busy café in

San Telmo, in which I had to excuse myself to throw up the panini I had just been eating while basically talking about myself for the previous half an hour. I do blame Quilmes for lots of things, but that's definitely one of them. I wonder if it made it into his publication. I also went to the city's famous Calle Florida, to source a few CDs of Sumo and I managed to pick up their famous album *Dividos Por La Felicidad* (meaning Divided By The Joy - or if you will Joy Division). I still play it regularly to this day.

Back in Ireland, national newspaper The Star ran a full page article on my exploits with Boca. SportsJoe ran a big story on it also. National radio broadcaster 2FM rang me up and interviewed me during a prime time slot. I got invited on an RTE radio show in their studio with legendary broadcaster Des Cahill and former Republic of Ireland manager Brian Kerr. I must say this: Brian Kerr's brain is a sponge of knowledge on football. I was flabbergasted with how much he knew about the game. He was telling me about some of Boca's youth players. This guy is no amateur. He was also incredibly lovely, and I was amazed he even knew who I was. We spoke about Boca, and Argentinian football in general, before Kerr shifted the topic onto music of which he is a big fan. He likened "Dale Boca Juniors" to the Stiff Little Fingers. That's a compliment I'll take all day long.

Twelve months later, I recorded a follow up single, titled "Bostero". I feel it's a better song that name-checks legends such as Maradona and Riquelme and has a very catchy chorus, but the media hype over the South Atlantic wasn't the same as what "Dale Boca Juniors" had generated. It didn't chart. Streaming was coming in at this point, so earning money from recorded music was slowly fading away. But that didn't stop another invite to Buenos Aires. So back over I went. I played the Temple Bar and filled it up again. I also played the legendary Liverpool Club in Palermo. Although I didn't sell it out, I was delighted it was very busy. Jet lag was very strong and I couldn't enjoy either gig, so I turned to Quilmes to help me sleep, which of course, made me quite ill.

THANKS TO THE BEAUTY of the internet, I am able to watch every Boca match live. I do to this day. Sometimes I can't. Sometimes I am onstage DJing at my long-standing residency in The Workmans Club in Dublin, so I get notifications from LiveScore keeping me up to date. I interact with fans online a lot. Specifically Twitter, or whatever that billionaire is calling it now. During the "Dale Boca Juniors" era, my notifications would be rammed. I'd also receive tons of abusive messages from fans of River, or as we like to call them RiBer. One time I gave River captain Leonardo Ponzio a bit of stick over his beard via Twitter. Ludicrously, it made newspaper headlines in Argentina.

When Boca faced River in Madrid in the 2018 Copa Libertadores final, I was offered free tickets from Boca fans who couldn't afford to travel to the Spanish capital. Personal circumstances at the time prevented me from going, but it was probably just as well, as hotel chains in the city had raised their prices by about 400%, but I never forgot that generosity.

I found out recently via a news article sent to me that a young couple, a Mexican man and an Argentinian woman, had met because of my very many tweets about Boca. They both had been commenting on one of my tweets. They noticed each other and then met up. They started dating. They eventually married and now have a daughter. All that from replying to me when I'm half cut, watching Boca at 2am, and tweeting semi-coherent sentiments about Cavani or whoever? Glad I'm here to help.

Some years back, when on holiday in Mallorca, with my wife and my daughter, I got a message from the Consulado Boca Juniors Mallorca. Basically they wanted to meet me and present me with a shirt on camera at my hotel. I was in the sweltering Balearic heat with a hangover, but agreed nonetheless. I met Mariano Valdés. A quiet, generous yet passionate Boca fan from Argentina and the president of the supporters club. He lives and breathes the club and his knowledge on the club's history amazes me. He's a family man who lives in Valldemossa, and always gives me the time of day, especially when I was researching for this book. His brother is involved with the Consulado in Barcelona, and I've met them too when they also presented me with their merchandise on camera. Their generosity moved me.

I've since travelled to Mallorca and attended a few events for Mariano's Consulado, including DJing pre-match before a Super-clásico in a nightclub in Can Pastilla, as well as attending a boister-ous party (where I also DJ'd briefly) for the Consulado, in a club in Cala Major, just outside Palma. The one thing I always take away from attending is, yes, it can seem boisterous and intimidating from the outside, but it would be hard to find nicer people. I assure you. They welcome me, a gringo from Ireland who chooses Guinness over an *asado* every time, into their group and with open arms? They treat me like royalty cause I make a bit of music? Why?

The answer is simple: "Somos soldados de Boca," as Mariano told me.

We are all soldiers of Boca.

Acknowledgements

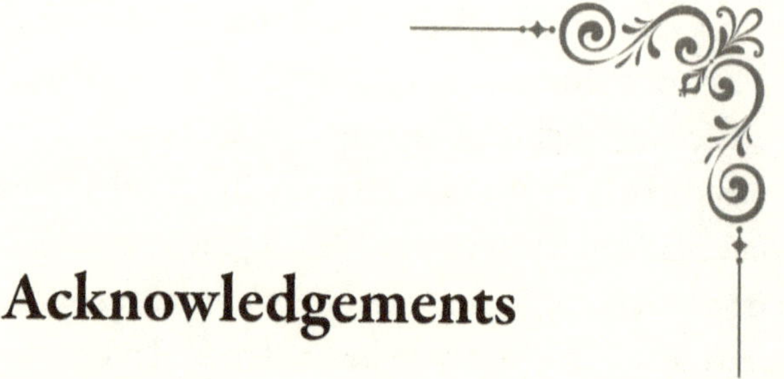

I would like to express my heartfelt thanks to Mariano Valdes for his unwavering guidance and deep passion for Boca. To Sergio Lodise and Leandro Cordobez, two wonderful historians whose tireless dedication to verifying the facts made this book all the more accurate and vibrant and without their help, this project would not have been as good as it is. My thanks also go to Consulado Boca Juniors de Mallorca for their passion and warm welcome they always give me, and to Felipe Bastitta for the striking photograph gracing the front cover. To Fiona and Frankie, for their love and patience that kept me grounded throughout this journey. And to all the bosteros around the globe, who continue to fuel my own passion with theirs, and to the supporters I've met in different cities, always welcoming me with open arms. Somos soldados de Boca.

Illustrations by: Bobby Turbulente.

Other photography by: Prensa Boca Juniors, Mariano Mortone, Sebastián Arce, Spike Bostero. Some photographs used are public domain.

About the Author

Rob Smith is a musician, DJ, producer and occasional writer. He has held a longstanding residency in the acclaimed Dublin music venue, The Workman's Club. He has performed or spun records around the globe, from Berlin to Buenos Aires and from Newcastle to New York. He releases records under the guise The Swedish Railway Orchestra, currently signed to Blowtorch Records. He lives in Ireland with his wife and daughter.